A HISTORY OF
BENEZETTE

HEART OF THE PENNSYLVANIA WILDS

KATHY MYERS

THE
History
PRESS

Published by The History Press
Charleston, SC
www.historypress.com

Copyright © 2024 by Kathy Myers
All rights reserved

Front cover, top: Guests at the wedding of Eva Winslow and Harvey Smith, June 29, 1904, at the home of her parents, W.K. and Mary Winslow. *Kathy Myers Collection. Bottom*: Fred Jr. bugling, 2005. *Willard C. Hill.*
Back cover: Table Falls on Paige Run. *Pennsylvania Great Outdoors Visitors Bureau.*

First published 2024

Manufactured in the United States

ISBN 9781467157230

Library of Congress Control Number: 2024930891

In memory of my ancestors, Winslow, Hicks and Smith,
early settlers of Elk and Cameron Counties in the Pennsylvania Wilds.

—❦—

Remember the days of old; consider the years of many generations;
ask your father, and he will show you, your elders, and they will tell you.
—Deuteronomy 32:7

CONTENTS

PREFACE

The Pennsylvania Wilds is a special place in America, with fifty state game lands, twenty-nine state parks, nine state and national forests and sixteen thousand miles of streams and rivers....The Pennsylvania Wilds [is] home to seventy percent of our nation's finest headwaters [and] to many people and industries who are able to make their living from the woods....It is also one of the largest expanses of green between New York City and Chicago.[1]

The Village of Benezette is ground zero for the elk herd in the Pennsylvania Wilds. One might say that Benezette is the heart of the Pennsylvania Wilds. But before it became well known for Pennsylvania's wild elk herd, it was a quiet village of hardworking individuals going about their daily lives. The Benezette region's first settler and his son arrived around 1787. From those small beginnings, eventually, a thriving community was built. As years passed, logging, railroads, coal and the discovery of natural gas all contributed to the economy of the region. This book details the history of Benezette and other nearby villages from the late 1700s through today.

ACKNOWLEDGEMENTS

Special thanks to the following people and organizations that have generously provided historical information, news articles and photographs to bring together this story of an area very dear to my heart.

John Bartholme, owner of Medix Run Lodges and the Fred Bartholme Memorial Chapel, for providing information about the creation of the chapel.

Cameron County Historical Society and three of its dedicated members, Susan Hoy, Dianne DeShong and Glenda (Neenan) Card, for historical documents, newspaper clippings and photos.

DuBois Area Historical Society for the use of its photos.

Elk County Historical Society for the use of its photos.

Edward Ferraro, attorney at law, Brockway, Pennsylvania, for an interview about the Medix Run gas boom.

Joshua Fox, curator, Pennsylvania Lumber Museum, for providing photos from Lumber Museum, Pennsylvania Historic and Museum Commission.

Willard C. Hill, outdoor photographer (https://pawildlifephotographer.blogspot.com), for the use of his photos of Old Fred, Bull No. 36.

Margie Leonard, Weedville, Pennsylvania, for sharing *Bennetts Valley News* photos.

Brenda Maholtz, Benezette, Pennsylvania, for providing a photo of the old Benezette store.

Bill McMahon, DuBois, Pennsylvania, for information about the project known as the Cross on the Hill.

Andrew Myers, MA, Registered Professional Archaeologist, Kane, Pennsylvania, for historic 1855 Benezette map.

Bert Reis, Medix Run, Pennsylvania, for historical data regarding General Potter's Big Elk Lick.

Taylor Tretick of Benezette Wines for providing a news story about Old Fred, Bull No. 36.

And to my husband, John Myers, thank you for your support, including all the photographs and the sites you visited with me to bring this book together.

INTRODUCTION

The sleepy Village of Benezette, in recent years, has become a focal point in the Pennsylvania Wilds for outdoor enthusiasts. As advertised on its web page, Visit PA Great Outdoors, people are invited to stop by.

> *Discover Benezette....Benezette is the "Elk Capital of Pennsylvania" and is located in the heart of the state's wild elk herd, now numbering nearly 1,400 majestic animals. The best spot to start an elk viewing adventure is at the Elk Country Visitor Center on Winslow Hill.*[2]

The Keystone Elk Country Alliance manages the visitor center and notes that it "sees upward of 480,000 visitors each year."[3]

"Let's go to Benezette" is an expression that has made the region a designation as much as it is a destination, with visitors roaming around the many small villages near Benezette. Weedville, Caledonia, Medix Run, Summerson, Grant, Dents Run, Hicks Run, Castle Garden, Driftwood and Sinnemahoning are all popular locations with visitors to the region. Winslow Hill, just outside the Village of Benezette, home to the Elk Country Visitor Center, offers a major elk viewing area; Mt. Zion Historic Park off Gray Hill Road was developed to recognize and preserve the history of the area on the site of the former Mt. Zion Church, the first Protestant church in Elk County; and the Quehanna Wild Area, accessed by the Quehanna Highway, is nearly fifty thousand acres of protected wildlife area, home to several species of birds and other animals, including elk, deer and coyotes.[4]

Welcome to Benezette, Elk Capital of Pennsylvania. *John Myers.*

Testimonials on Facebook provide first-person acknowledgement of the region's popularity:

> *Oh how I miss Elk Country, we ride up on our Harley several times a year in spring and fall. Love it.*

> *Never gets old, even after twenty years.*

> *Another little bit of heaven on earth! Love* [Benezette] *and the great folks who live there!*

> *We love the area and make a trip up every year from WV.... Thanks y'all for the wonderful hospitality we always receive. Good peoples.*

Before the region became the Elk Capital of Pennsylvania, Benezette was a "peaceful and quiet village."[5] It is its history and that of other nearby villages from the earliest days to the present time that is offered in this book.

Chapter 1

HISTORY OF
THE BENEZETTE WILDS

To understand the settlement of the region of Pennsylvania known as the Wilds requires a look back at the history of the Commonwealth of Pennsylvania following the American Revolution.

When the Treaty of Paris ending hostilities between the United States and Britain was signed on September 3, 1783, this country's boundaries extended west to the Mississippi River, north to Canada with fishing rights in Newfoundland and south to Florida. What the treaty did not address was the rights of the Native Americans who had fought on the side of the British. In 1784, the United States government offered a treaty at Fort Stanwix to the Iroquois Confederacy. Ratified by the United States in 1785, it was never ratified by the Indians.[6] It included the surrender of Indian lands that make up a twenty-three-county area in western Pennsylvania, which became known as the Last Purchase of 1784. The twelve and a half counties that compose the Wilds were contained in that treaty.

THE NATIVE AMERICANS

In the history of Elk County there is a story, very possibly a local legend, of one early settler, a pioneer hunter by the name of General Wade, and his family, who, along with a friend named Slade, came to the headwaters of the Little Toby Creek in 1798, settling there temporarily. As the story goes, the party returned east in 1803. By 1806, having come again to the area, it is recounted that Wade and Slade interacted with an Indian girl at a place known as Blue Rock. The girl was introduced to Mrs. Wade and eventually became the wife of Slade, married by Chief Tamsqua. The legend goes on to describe the interaction of Slade and Tamsqua with the White settlers when they arrived, smoking the peace pipe with them.[7]

In reality, there was little contact between White settlers and Native Americans in the area surrounding Benezette in the years following the Last Purchase of 1784, after the American Revolution and the opening of this region to settlers. The Cornplanter Grant, which was located in what eventually became Warren County, was given to Cornplanter, a Seneca chief, by the Pennsylvania government for his policies of reconciliation following the hostilities of the Revolution and subsequent skirmishes.[8]

In an earlier time, however, the Sinnemahoning Creek, and by extension the Bennett's Branch, were the sites of small Indian villages or hunting camps. "The name, Sinnemahoning, is a corruption of Achsinni-mahoni, or 'stony lick.' An Indian trail ran up the West Branch [Susquehanna River] from Shamokin (Sunbury) to the Big Island (Lock Haven), and then on up the West Branch, along the northern shore to the Sinnemahoning….This trail later became the pathway of the early settlers."[9]

Near Medix Run, within Benezette Township, by a spring, is a stone mill that was used by the Native Americans to grind corn into flour. Over the years, artifacts such as arrowheads, flint knives, tomahawks and other flint objects have been found, including near the ball field in Benezette.[10]

In nearby Sinnemahoning, there is evidence that Indian villages stood on the flats near the mouth of First Fork. Flooding in 1848 and 1861 exposed wigwam chimneys in rows. In 1877, while digging a ditch in Sinnemahoning, the remains of an Indian were unearthed: a small portion of skull and remaining bones. Blue beads, a clay pipe and other artifacts were found there as well. An Indian cemetery was located on Bennett's Branch. In Sterling Run, Cameron County, while excavating for a new post office in 1873, seventeen skeletons were uncovered.[11]

THE *JOURNAL OF SAMUEL MACLAY*

In 1790, the Supreme Executive Council of Pennsylvania directed three men, Samuel Maclay, Timothy Matlack and John Adlum, to begin an expedition into the West Branch of the Susquehanna River, Sinnemahoning

Creek and the Allegheny River to find a possible route for a road to connect the Allegheny River with the West Branch of the Susquehanna River. The expedition physically began on April 26, 1790. Part of this five-month journey, described in the *Journal of Samuel Maclay*, directly relates to the Benezette region:

> *From Philadelphia to the Forks of the Sinnemahoning, 326 miles*
> *Up the West Branch of the Sinnemahoning, 24 miles.*[12]

In addition to Maclay, Matlack and Adlum, three other men were along as guides: Thomas Semor, Gershom Hicks and Matthew Gray. It is Gershom Hicks who left a lasting mark on the Benezette region—he is credited by one historian with naming Hicks Run.[13]

Hicks had an interesting background. In 1755, during the French and Indian War, the Delaware Indians, under the leadership of Shingas, attacked an area in southern Pennsylvania, near today's McConnellsburg, known as the Big Cove, the Little Cove and the Tonolloways. In what was recorded in history as the Great Cove Massacre, a number of settlers were killed. Among the dead were John Hicks and his son, while his wife, Barbara, and four other sons were taken captive. Barbara Hicks was rescued by Colonel Armstrong's raid on Kittanning, Pennsylvania, in 1756, when she was being held with a number of other captives. Most likely, her sons were held there as well. Gershom Hicks and his brother Levi were in captivity until about 1761, and their two other brothers, Moses and one unnamed, were captives until a peace treaty was signed in 1765. It was said by people who knew Gershom and Levi in those later years that they retained their Indian ways once they returned from captivity.[14]

Gershom Hicks went on to serve his country during the American Revolution, when he undertook a spying mission for George Washington; Hicks was the only one on the mission to return. He crossed southern New York State from Niagara to Chemung and reported his findings

The *Journal of Samuel Maclay*, 1790. Published by John G. Meginness, 1887.

to Washington. His work enabled General Sullivan to make a raid on the Indian tribes and British soldiers in New York State.[15]

The *Journal of Samuel Maclay* describes the group of explorers living off the land, carrying only basic amounts of provisions with them. Traveling from the West Branch of the Susquehanna, they rowed their canoes up the Sinnemahoning Creek.[16] Meginness, who published Maclay's journal in 1894, noted, "There were no white settlers in this section. It was a very wild place—in fact, a 'howling wilderness.'"[17]

On June 14, they arrived at what is today known as the Bennett's Branch of the Sinnemahoning Creek or, in an earlier time, Second Fork. Bennett's Branch was named for John Bennett, possibly the only White settler in the region.

By June 15, the party had pushed on to Bennett's cabin, where they camped for the night. With the morning of the seventeenth cloudy and provisions running low, one of the guides, Semor, shot at a doe elk. The doe was wounded, and Semor and Hicks went to find it. Maclay's journal describes the party hunting at "elk licks," salt licks that attracted wildlife. One such lick was located near the mouth of Trout Run at Benezette where, in later years, salt was manufactured.[18]

Eventually, the group left the region surrounding Bennett's cabin, climbing a mountain on an old Indian trail and making their way off to the distant Toby's Creek. Eventually arriving at Big Toby's Creek, today known as the Clarion River, they reached an area near what is now Ridgway, the county seat of Elk County.[19]

Gershom's nephew Levi Hicks Jr., along with Samuel Smith and Andrew Overturf, settled in Cameron County in 1806.[20]

General James Potter and The Big Elk Lick

Traveling east from Medix Run on Route 555, at the edge of the Village of Benezette, a sign has been erected that reads, "Gen'l Potter's The Big Elk Lick 1785," located on a portion of land that was awarded to General James Potter for his service in the American Revolution. The 379½ acres was warranted and patented as "The Big Elk Lick," with that designation appearing in the early Clearfield County Court House records.

Potter was born in County Tyrone, Ireland, and, along with his family, immigrated to New Castle, Delaware, in 1741. Eventually the family settled

General Potter's The Big Elk Lick at Benezette, Pennsylvania. *John Myers.*

in Cumberland County, Pennsylvania. Growing up in what was at that time the Pennsylvania frontier, Potter did not receive a formal education.[21] He became a lieutenant in the militia and at age twenty-five, during the French and Indian War, was with Armstrong at the Battle of Kittanning to rescue settlers who had been captured by the Delaware Indians. After the treaty of 1768, more land became available for settlement, and he was appointed commissioner by the provincial government to encourage settlement in Penns Valley.[22]

Potter served through the American Revolution as a colonel and was a member of the Constitutional Convention in Philadelphia. He became lieutenant governor of Pennsylvania and served as an ex officio trustee of the University of Pennsylvania. Potter became a major general in 1782 and a deputy surveyor for Pennsylvania in Northumberland County in 1785.[23] The warrant for the property he acquired in what is now Elk County was also dated 1785.

Bert Reis, who operated The Big Elk Lick Horse Campground at Benezette for over twenty years and is patriarch of the Reis family now operating the campground, was from Pittsburgh and a salesman for 3M Company. His sales territory in this area included companies in Ridgway, St. Marys and Penfield. Eventually relocating to this region, he once served as a Benezette

Township supervisor, and with his many interests, he is very knowledgeable about the history of his adopted home.

When Reis acquired the property that had been a portion of what was known as The Big Elk Lick, he wanted to learn more about its history, including the chain of title back through the years and its naming. History records that General James Potter sold the land to early settler Leonard Morey in 1815. Morey in turn sold the property to Reuben Winslow.[24] The date of the sale of the property to Morey is somewhat puzzling, as General Potter died in 1789. It is more likely that Morey purchased the land from the heirs of General Potter. Researching the deeds in the Clearfield County Court House, Reis found references to the original warrant, dated May 4, 1785, and the patent, dated June 18, 1810, for the acreage known as The Big Elk Lick. The patent and warrant were recorded on April 26, 1831. He also found a deed from James and William Potter, executors of the estate of General James Potter, deceased, to George Winslow, again for the acreage referred to as The Big Elk Lick, for the consideration of $2,000, including all improvements, houses, barn and stable, also recorded on April 26, 1831. Apparently, those were the improvements made by Leonard Morey, who failed to acquire title to the land.

The George Winslow mentioned in the deed was Reuben Winslow's older brother who was a sea captain and lived in Malden, Massachusetts. George Winslow had retired from the sea in 1830 after having sailed out of Boston for many years trading with Europe and China. His last command found him stationed at Lintin, China, where he remained for three years prior to retirement.[25]

While it's unknown why George Winslow received title to The Big Elk Lick from the estate of General Potter, one can speculate. Did he come into the region in 1831 to buy land, intending to settle near his brothers? Or with free time on his hands after retirement, returning to his home in Massachusetts, might he have taken the opportunity to visit his elderly mother, who was living in Punxsutawney? Another guess: George wasn't planning on relocating from Massachusetts, but while he was visiting his mother, the property came up for sale. If he didn't buy it for himself, was big brother George a go-between when Reuben may have been low on funds? By purchasing the property, which was later deeded over to Reuben, he helped his younger brother to eventually gain the land and buildings that had belonged to Leonard Morey. A recent review of the records shows a deed from George Winslow and Elizabeth Winslow, his wife, transferring The Big Elk Lick to Reuben Winslow, recorded in Clearfield County on March 15, 1836.

It is likely that The Big Elk Lick is the same lick described in the *Journal of Samuel Maclay* near the mouth of Trout Run at Benezette.

Today, it is not unusual to find elk trekking across Route 555 from the bottomland near the creek, to the other side of the road very near where the "Gen'l Potter's The Big Elk Lick 1785" sign is located. Reading about The Big Elk Lick Horse Campground, one learns it provides a wilderness opportunity for those who enjoy riding horses: "Bring your own horses to camp and ride the trails through the wilderness in the heart of the Benezette elk herd with access to Thunder Mountain Equestrian Trail."[26] As noted in the earlier account by Maclay, it's an opportunity to ride through "a howling wilderness"—or, at least in today's jargon, a bugling wilderness during the annual elk rut in the fall of the year.

Chapter 2

THE FOUNDING OF BENEZETTE

THE LEGEND OF BENEZETTE

Long ago, when the Indians were still there, a white family lived where the town now stands. The white family had a little boy named Bennie and Bennie went into the woods and got lost. Everyone hunted for Bennie—even the Indians helped, but the child could not be found. One Indian, looking very sad, said to the father and mother, "Bennie's et," meaning a bear had eaten Bennie. Repeating it many times to all who gathered, it soon became Bennieset or Bennezett.[27]

WHY DID THE SETTLERS COME AND HOW DID THEY GET HERE?

The Last Purchase of 1784 afforded investors the opportunity to purchase lands for development. The Holland Land Company was an unincorporated syndicate of thirteen Dutch investors from Amsterdam. As aliens were forbidden to own land in the United States, the investors placed their funds in the hands of trustees who bought land in western New York State and western Pennsylvania. The syndicate hoped to sell land rapidly. It began advertising large tracts of land in the region known as the Wilds.

75,000 Acres of Land
Will be sold at Public Sale to the
Highest Bidder

The Holland Land-company, desirous to promote the Settlement and Population of the interior parts of the State, and open the Sale of their Lands in the 6 east Allegany Districts, offer 75 tracts of land, containing about 990 acres each, at Public Sale. These lands are situated in the 3ᵈ or Canan's District, and in the Counties of McKean and Clearfield [the Benezette region was at that time part of Clearfield County], *near the navigable Waters of the Susquehanna. The soil is good and well-watered by several Streams, vis. The Sinnemahoning and Kockeketow Creek, and Bennet's Branch (some of them boatable) falling into the West Branch of the Susquehanna. A good Wagon Road has been opened from the mouth of the Bald Eagle Creek, on the West Branch of the Susquehanna, up the navigable Waters of the Sinnemahoning to Driftwood, and thence continued in a northwesterly direction, to the State line.*[28]

REUBEN COLBURN WINSLOW, FOUNDER OF BENEZETTE

Reuben Colburn Winslow was a native of Maine, born in 1796, who, along with his parents, Carpenter and Elizabeth Colburn Winslow, and four brothers, immigrated to the Punxsutawney area in Jefferson County prior to 1818.[29] His father had been a shipbuilder in Wiscasset, Maine, and his mother was the daughter of Major Reuben Colburn, who, at George Washington's instruction, supplied "batteaux" or flat-bottomed boats for Benedict Arnold's raid into Canada in 1775, just prior to the Revolution. Winslow had four additional brothers who were sea captains and remained in Maine and Massachusetts. Reuben Colburn Winslow married Elizabeth Collins of Curwensville, Clearfield County, Pennsylvania, on November 15, 1818.[30]

While no historical record has been found of why the Winslow family uprooted and came into the Wilds, an advertisement that appeared in the *United States Gazette* in 1817 certainly was enticing:

FOR SALE
Thirty Thousand acres of Valuable Land, in Jefferson and Venango counties, Pennsylvania, formerly the property of the Holland Land

Company. To be sold on a credit of several years—or very cheap for cash. For terms apply to **HENRY SHIPPEN,** *Lancaster, August 2, 1817.*[31]

Land! The family set out from Maine by ship on the Atlantic Ocean, sailing south to the Chesapeake Bay. Following the bay north to Havre de Grace, where the Susquehanna River enters the bay, the family made its way via the river to Harrisburg. Taking the West Branch of the Susquehanna, they eventually arrived in Clearfield, Pennsylvania, where they rested. Preparing to move on, they built a bridge across the water, near Curwensville, making the final journey overland following an Indian trail, the Great Shamokin Path, and arriving at their destination near present-day Punxsutawney in Jefferson County.[32]

Eventually, Reuben Winslow, along with two of his brothers, Carpenter Winslow Jr. and Ebenezer Winslow, relocated from Punxsutawney to Benezette. Reuben Winslow acquired 379½ acres of land and, by 1844, had laid out town lots.[33] Winslow is credited with naming the village Benezette, although for years it was shown on maps as Winslow.

While one might assume the name Benezette was somehow a way to "fancify" the name of early settler John Bennett, for whom the Bennett's Branch of Sinnemahoning Creek (where the village is located) was named, a newspaper article that appeared in the *Elk County Advocate* in 1881 claimed that Winslow chose the surname of Anthony Benezet, a French American abolitionist and educator from Philadelphia.[34] There may be some veracity to the theory that he chose the name of Benezet, an avowed abolitionist, as Winslow's grandfather James Winslow was a Quaker and many Quakers were involved in the abolitionist movement. There is evidence that Winslow's two brothers who remained in the Punxsutawney area were active in the Underground Railroad. Joseph Wood Winslow, at Hudson, just outside of town, provided a station for fugitive slaves, and his brother Judge James Winslow along with James's son-in-law, James Minish, operated stations and were conductors in Punxsutawney.[35] In 1963, when the Minish house at 504 Mahoning Street, Punxsutawney, was being demolished, a "slave pit" was uncovered: a place where fugitive slaves were hidden in an underground twelve-foot-by-twelve-foot room with earthen floors and three side walls, with the fourth outside wall being the foundation of the house.[36]

Reuben Winslow became an extensive landowner, purchasing several hundred acres in and around Benezette. He served as one of Elk County's first commissioners in 1843.[37] He was elected a school director in the first township election in 1844 and was a prominent merchant.[38] He had also

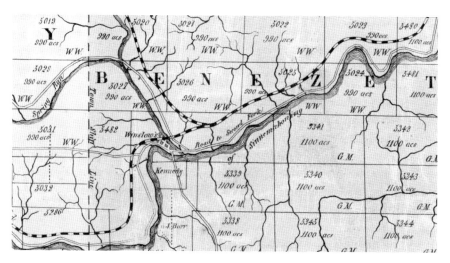

Map showing the town of Winslow, 1855. *Library of Congress.*

served as prothonotary (which included the office of register and recorder) of Clearfield County, of which Elk was then part, in 1825.[39]

In 1861, Winslow was active in recruiting soldiers for the storied Civil War Bucktail Regiment, along with his nephew Thomas B. Winslow, forming the Elk County Rifles.

Winslow's business interests were widespread, and he was involved in coal, lumbering and railroading. He was killed in a train wreck near Lock Haven in 1871.[40]

Benezette reached its peak in growth around 1910. As the settlers took root, the town grew rapidly. In 1850, Benezette Township, which included Medix Run, Benezette, Summerson, Grant and Dents Run, counted thirty-six dwellings, thirty-six families, 243 inhabitants, twenty farms and ten industries, most located near Benezette. In Benezette itself, by 1870, "E.E. Fletcher and William Johnson were merchants; two blacksmiths, T. Guilfoyle and H.D. Derr, served the people; the lumbermen were D.B. Winslow, B.E. Mowrey and R.W. Doyle. In addition, there were painters, farmers and saloon keepers. About that time the town boasted of such hotels as the 'Benezette' owned by Henry Blesh, the 'Winslow' and the 'Daley.'"[41] In 1884, a fire swept through the town, destroying the business section and eleven homes. With a strong pioneer spirit, that same year, the Independent Order of Odd Fellows Hall was built, and construction on the Blesh and Son General Store was begun; the store opened for business in 1885.[42] The store was still in operation in 1980, during which year there were approximately

Left: Benezette: the heart of Pennsylvania's Elk Country. *Pennsylvania Great Outdoors Visitors Bureau.*

Middle: Fourth of July celebration at the IOOF (Independent Order of Odd Fellows) Hall, Benezette, circa 1920. *Kathy Myers collection.*

Bottom: Hazelnut Cottage, now on the site of the former Benezette store. *John Myers.*

Top: Hazelnut Cottage sign. *John Myers.*

Bottom: Benezette Hotel. *John Myers.*

Benezette Store following a fire in 1999. *Brenda Maholtz.*

165 people living in fifty-two homes. The town boasted a hotel, two stores, two churches and a post office.[43] The 2020 census, again reporting all of Benezette Township, revealed 227 people, 104 households and sixty-six families in those five villages listed earlier.[44]

EARLY SETTLERS

Axes and hoes were clumsily made by the rough blacksmith. Grain and hay were stacked in the fields or yard or put into round log barns. Threshing was done with flail or trampled out with oxen or horses; the grain was separated from the chaff by winnowing it through the meshes of a riddle....Corn and buckwheat were sometimes ground on hand mills and sifted through sieves made from dressed perforated sheep or deer skins....Major Bennett who made an improvement on the Potter reserve at Benezette...yoked his milch cows to plough his garden and his fields.[45]

The earliest settlers began coming into the Benezette region around 1785–87 when the United States was still in its infancy. Consider the newly formed country in those years. Growing from the post–Revolutionary War period, in 1787, the United States did not have a president; rather, under the direction of George Washington, the men assigned to the Constitutional Convention were involved in writing the United States Constitution. That effort was followed by the ratification process.[46] In 1789, George Washington was elected the first president, serving two terms until 1797.[47] In 1800, the U.S. capital was changed from Philadelphia to the newly formed District of Columbia. In 1803, the United States purchased the Louisiana Territory from France, greatly expanding the country from the Mississippi River to the Rocky Mountains: 830,000 square miles for $15 million. Lewis and Clark began their expedition to reach the Pacific Ocean in 1804, arriving on the West Coast in 1805. In 1812, war began between Britain and the United States, ending in 1814. By 1815, the country had entered a period in history known as the Era of Good Feelings, when U.S. citizens started to pay less attention to European political and military matters—what many today would refer to as isolationism.[48]

What follows are thumbnail sketches of some of the earliest settlers into the region.

John Bennett

There are two historical accounts of John Bennett. The *Journal of Samuel Maclay* notes that the Bennett's Branch of the Sinnemahoning Creek was named for him and that he arrived in the area from Lycoming County about 1785.[49] The other version of the story is that he arrived with his father from Lycoming County in 1787 to hunt beaver and that they built a cabin near Caledonia and continued trapping until 1796. Another source claims that William Bennett arrived in the region in 1810 or 1811 and settled where Benezette is located—William was possibly the aforementioned father of John Bennett.[50]

One early settler in the region visited Bennett's main cabin near the mouth of Trout Run in 1814, noting that the corn hills planted by him were visible and that he also had another cabin near Driftwood.[51] History records that John Bennett died in 1841 in Lycoming County.[52]

Dr. Daniel Rogers

Dr. Daniel Rogers was perhaps the first doctor to enter the region that became known as Benezette Township. He arrived in the autumn of 1811 as the land agent for Shippen, McMurtrie & Co., landowners of approximately one hundred thousand acres lying in what are now Elk and Clearfield Counties. The handbill that Shippen, McMurtrie & Co. produced presented the region and its potential for settlers in glowing terms.

> *It is confidently believed that, taking into consideration the situation, soil and general advantages that belong to this tract, there seldom has existed a more favorable opportunity for industrious and enterprising men to acquire a handsome property upon more liberal terms.... The subscribers purchased the property after a full and complete inspection of the soil and other local advantages, and a satisfactory investigation of the title. It is intended for the present to sell to actual settlers at two dollars per acre, at a credit of five years, two years without interest.*[53]

Dr. Rogers cleared lands and built a cabin, sixteen by twenty feet, where early settlers found shelter on their arrival. The historical record provides no information about his practice of medicine. After a few years in Benezette Township, he moved to the Jersey Shore to pursue his medical career.[54]

Leonard and Balfour Erasmus Morey

In July 1879, a ceremony was held in Ridgway, the county seat of Elk County, for the placement of a cornerstone for the newly designed courthouse, which is the building standing today. Honored guests at that ceremony included Erasmus Morey, who had been in Elk County since 1813 and was, at his death in 1891, described as the county's oldest resident.[55] "He witnessed the growth of the county from the time it was a wilderness until the present day. He is 83 years old and cannot give expression to his feelings in words."[56] The words Morey wrote for the courthouse ceremony were read aloud:

> *Gentlemen Commissioners: I return my sincere thanks for your invitation to be present at the laying of the corner-stone of the court house, and to take so prominent a part in the proceedings. It is one of the days of my life, long to be remembered, and my wish is that you may get us up a good substantial building, that will last for many generations to come; that we may have impartial justice administered to all parties that may have litigations within its walls.*[57]

Erasmus Morey was the son of Leonard Morey, one of the first settlers of Benezette. Leonard, born in 1771 in Woodstock, Connecticut, was the son of a Revolutionary War solder.

In 1812, after seeing a handbill printed by the Holland Land Company advertising land in McKean and Clearfield Counties, Leonard set off to view the region. Apparently impressed by what he saw, in late February 1813, he brought his family into the wilderness. In 1815, he purchased 379½ acres near the mouth of Trout Run in Benezette from lands of General James Potter. Morey erected a gristmill there and a log house for himself, his wife, his invalid mother-in-law and his five children. Morey spent a lot of time attending to the gristmill, which ground seven or eight bushels a day. In 1822, he cut and made a road from Karthaus to the Bennett's Branch, receiving twelve dollars a mile.[58] His wife died in 1826, and one year later, he sold his land. Morey and his wife are both buried at the Benezette Cemetery.

In 1824, Leonard's son Erasmus Morey married Mary Weed, whose family were pioneers at Weedville. They settled near Benezette. Erasmus served as postmaster and was a staunch Republican.[59] He spent his early years hunting and fighting Indians.[60] Successful in farming and in business, he had one of the finest farms in the township, developed from the wilderness where he arrived as a seventeen-year-old.

Erasmus Morey died on May 25, 1891, and is buried at Mt. Zion Cemetery not far from Benezette. His obituary, carried in the *Valley Echo*, chronicled his life. "During the long stretch of 78 years living in these parts, it was Father Morey's privilege to witness a wonderful change from dense forest to complete civilization. He had brought the lumber for his coffin to Mr. Avery and had arranged his monument at Mt. Zion. But his best monument was a well lived life."[61]

THE LEWIS FAMILY

Lewis Lewis, also known as William Lewis, immigrated to America before the Revolution, locating in York County, Pennsylvania. He was the first surveyor in Centre County, Pennsylvania, when it was still part of Northumberland County. He became deputy surveyor of all the land in Northumberland County. Surveying was a dangerous occupation in those early days because of Indians and wild animals. Other areas he surveyed were along the Susquehanna River; the Bald Eagle Creek, where Milesburg is located; and along the Juniata River, where he laid out the town of Lewistown, which was named after him.[62]

Lewis Lewis's son, Thomas Lewis, visited Elk County in 1804 along with a surveyor named Webb. In 1811, he came into the region again, stopping for a time at Driftwood to raise a crop of corn. He returned to Bellefonte, but this region apparently held a fascination for him, and in December 1817, he moved his family, making the trip by canoe. They traveled up the Susquehanna River to Lock Haven, which was then known as Big Island. Continuing on to the Sinnemahoning Creek, they followed the creek to the Bennett's Branch. The area was rugged, with no roads.

Mr. and Mrs. Thomas Lewis raised a family of six children. Their oldest son, Ellis, was born in Bellefonte on January 1, 1808. Ellis had no opportunity to receive an education, as there were no schools in the Benezette region when they arrived. Working with his father, he learned the trade of millwright, continuing in that occupation for seven years. He married Annie Michaels in 1837, and they eventually became the parents of eleven children. By 1839, he had taken over his father's farm and was engaged in farming and lumbering. Over the years, he was elected county treasurer and held various local offices. [63]

It was an article in the *DuBois Courier-Express* in 1974 that brought additional attention to the early Lewis family. Jim Ross, a native of Medix Run, wrote an article titled "The Saga of the Lonesome Grave on Rock Hill." Rock Hill is located a mile west of Medix Run. In the article, Ross described the lonesome grave, noting, "For 132 years the occupant of this grave who at death was 108 years old, J.D. Lewis, has rested in peace high on the rugged mountain near the Lewis farm above Medix Run, Elk County, in what has been termed for years as 'The Lonesome Grave on Rock Hill.'"[64] Lewis's "peaceful rest" was soon to be disturbed by a coal-stripping project, Ross noted, and the timber that shaded the grave had been cut. Ross briefly reviewed the history of the Lewis family who settled that location, recalling that Rock Hill had been one of the "finest hunting areas in the Bennett's Valley and as the name suggests, very rough. There have been many black bears killed there through the years."[65] Visiting the grave site, Ross and a companion marked the inscription carved on the stone with chalk, revealing the name J.D. Lewis and the dates 1734–1842. He did not provide a clue as to the identity of J.D. Lewis in the Lewis family tree.

A search of Ancestry.com revealed that the wife of the early settler Lewis Lewis was Jane (Dill) Lewis Leathers-Stevens, and an article in the *Gettysburg Times* describing the history of early settlers mentions that Lewis Lewis, the surveyor, married Jane Dill, the fourth child of Thomas and Mary Dill, before June 1, 1769, at Carlisle. The article lists her birthdate as 1750, contradicting the date carved on the stone.[66] Jane's husband, Lewis Lewis, died in an accident while surveying, and she went on to marry again twice, both marriages ending in widowhood. The mystery of the lonesome grave is solved: she was the mother of Thomas Lewis, who apparently buried her under her first husband's surname. The grave has been clearly marked in recent years: "1750–1841, 91 years." Consider the history that Jane passed through in her life's journey: the French and Indian War, the American Revolution, the opening of the region known as the Wilds in 1784 and the War of 1812. Remembered as "vivacious and possessed of boundless energy, her reputation as a horsewoman… [clinging]…tenaciously to her memory," Jane Dill Lewis is at rest on Rock Hill.[67]

Chapter 3

NEARBY VILLAGES

Weedville

Weedville, July 11th, 1874

Dear Advocate—The Glorious Fourth has come and gone, and it was a great day for this place. In the morning it looked very much like rain, but notwithstanding the appearance of the weather by ten o'clock quite a number of people had assembled. There were two platforms erected, one for the speakers and one for dancing. About one o'clock a sumptuous dinner was served, there were all kinds of pies and cakes (all except buckwheat cakes) peaches, ice cream, etc., and everything went fine until the second table had ate when a shower arose and it began to hail, and hail fell larger than hen's eggs for about five minutes, after which there was another table set, and after all had partaken of a hearty meal, they prepared for a nice time of "tripping the light fantastic toe."[68]

The Benezette experience begins in Weedville, located in Jay Township, Elk County, the "western gateway" to the region, where State Route 555 runs between Elk and Cameron Counties, winding its way to the "eastern gateway," Sinnemahoning, along Route 120, providing a scenic drive through the Benezette Wilds.

The village takes its name from early settler Abijah Barnabus Weed, who, along with his wife, Charlotte Mead Weed, came to what is now Elk County from New York State in 1818. They raised a family of seven children.[69]

Welcome to the Elk Scenic Drive, Route 555. *John Myers.*

While the early Weed family was primarily involved in farming, it is recorded that in the spring of 1816, prior to the arrival of the Weed family, the first sawmill on the Bennett's Branch, located on Kersey Run in Weedville, was built by John Boyd. The first tannery in Elk County was built near Weedville sometime around 1820 by a Frederick Weed.[70] It is not known if he had a connection to the family for whom the village was named.

An earlier historian noted that "the village did not seem to grow until the coal mines were opened at the nearby villages."[71] In the most recent census, from 2020, the village's population was 460.

The introduction to this section, as recorded in the *Elk County Advocate*, about a "Glorious Fourth" seems appropriate for this community, as for many years, beginning in 1951, it has hosted the Bennett's Valley Homecoming on Labor Day. The sixty-eighth anniversary of the event was in 2019. After the COVID-19 pandemic restrictions in effect in 2020, 2021 and 2022 were lifted, the Bennett's Valley Homecoming was once again celebrated in September 2023.

CALEDONIA

But let me tell you that I love you, that I think about you all the time
Caledonia you're calling me and now I'm going home
For if I should become a stranger you know that it would make me more than sad
Caledonia's been everything I've ever had.[72]

According to historical records, "Caledonia was an area of north Britain beyond Roman control, roughly corresponding to modern Scotland."[73] The lyrics above, from a modern song, "Caledonia," were written by a man who was longing for his homeland of Scotland.

Finding no historical record for the naming of the village of Caledonia, one can speculate it had something to do with the ethnicity of its early settlers. Was it Caledonia from the beginning, or was there a name change at some time during its history? Its first recorded pioneers were Zebulon and Hezekiah Warner, Warner being an Anglo-Saxon name derived from a Germanic form.[74] Or perhaps the lay of the land, so to speak, reminded the early settlers of Scotland.

Another possible origin of the village's name may have been an early family who settled nearby, the Kincaids, "Kincaid" being of Scottish derivation. Is it possible that this early family may have influenced the naming of Caledonia?

Dr. Noah Kincaid and his wife, Lydia Hough Kincaid, arrived in Luzerne County, Pennsylvania, from New York State sometime around 1800. Both were natives of Connecticut, and Noah was a veteran of the War of 1812. Lydia's father was a veteran of the Revolutionary War. Both Noah and Lydia were descendants of early settlers in this country, Lydia's Hough line going back to Cheshire, England, and Noah's line going back to Scotland. One of Noah's ancestors was apparently a military man who had trouble with his superiors and was banished to the colonies, arriving in New Jersey around 1685.[75] Noah and Lydia arrived in the Wilds region in the 1820s. They were the parents of ten children. Lydia died in 1841 and is buried in the Kincaid Family Cemetery on Rock Hill Road between Caledonia and Medix Run. Noah eventually went to live with his daughter in Cameron County and died in 1858; he is buried at the Devling Farm Cemetery in Sterling Run.

Caledonia was a village of firsts. On November 6, 1843, the first Elk County court was ordered to be held in the home of Hezekiah Warner. In fact, court was held in a nearby building that was also a schoolhouse, a twenty-foot-by-twenty-four-foot building, on December 19, 1843, the same year Elk County was established.[76] By 1844, the court had been moved to Ridgway, which became the county seat.[77]

An official post office was established in 1828; mail was carried from Milesburg to Smethport once a week on horseback. The first road passing through Caledonia, the Caledonia Pike, was opened between Bellefonte and Meadville.

In 1827, a road was cut from Caledonia to the Ridgway area.[78] Caledonia's citizens were farmers but also involved in lumber and coke production, which are discussed in later chapters.

While "Caledonia" suggests a romantic or poetic name for ancient Scotland, there were two events in Elk County's Caledonia that were shocking—the murder of Constable Frank Wernith and the murder of Phebe Shopland Cochran.

DEFYING THE LAW

THE COLD-BLOODED MURDER OF CONSTABLE WERNITH
BY HARRY ENGLISH THE NOTED FORGER—
CONSTABLE VOLLMER WOUNDED[79]

The *Elk County Advocate* told the story of a killing by a man who was wanted on a charge of forgery and the men who went to serve a warrant for his arrest:

> *About 10:30 o'clock last Friday morning, Sheriff Oyster received a dispatch to the effect that Harry English had shot and killed Frank Wernith, constable of Benzinger Township, and wounded Philip Vollmer, constable of St. Marys Borough while these officers were endeavoring to arrest him.*
>
> *Three or four weeks ago detectives from Bradford, in company with Frank Wernith…tracked Harry English to the house of A.J. Rummer, his father-in-law, in Jay Township, where they arrested him on a charge of forgery, when he asked permission to go into another room on some trivial pretext, and succeeded in making good his escape, Constable Wernith sending several shots after the escaping prisoner but without effect.*
>
> *Constable Vollmer had received notice of Thursday last that English was again at the house of Rummer. District Attorney G.W. Wurzell, Thomas J. Burke, and Constable Vollmer were taken to Caledonia by young Kreig, stopping at Spring Run where Constable Wernith was working and took*

him in. The party reached their destination late at night and lay in a barn until just before daylight on Friday morning, when arrangements were made for the capture of English. Wurzell and Burke took positions where they could cover the rear of the house, while the two constables approached from the front and entered the house by two front doors. In about fifteen minutes English made his appearance, and on discovering the constables commenced to yell and ran up the stairs. Wernith followed in hot haste but was met at near the top with a kick which landed him at the foot again. On recovering himself he fired at English hitting him in the left leg, the ball going through the fleshy part of the leg and landing in the dress of Mrs. Rummer which hung on the wall. (Deputy Sheriff Wensel secured the bullet and carries it as a souvenir of the sad affair.) English ran into a bedroom and snatching up a sixteen-shooter Spencer rifle asked, "Where is that man?" The door was partly open as Wernith reached the upper floor the second time when English threw the door wide open and shot him through the body. After shooting the Benzinger constable, English walked across the room and fired at Vollmer who was some sixty or seventy feet from the house the shot taking effect in the lower portion of the body making an ugly wound although at last accounts the man was doing as well as could be expected under the circumstances. Mr. Rummer, who was asleep at the commencement of the fracas, soon got out of bed and just in time to throw up the Spencer rifle which was aimed at District Attorney Wurzell. Three times did the desperate man attempt to kill the latter, and three times was he foiled by the prompt action of the father-in-law. No doubt but for the interference of Mr. Rummer another murder would have been added to the list of the desperado's crimes.

Constable Wernith, after receiving the fatal shot, ran down stairs, outdoors and several feet from the house where he fell. Being assisted to his feet he walked nearly to the Caledonia house, some ten or twelve rods, when he again sank to the earth and was carried into the hotel. The shooting took place at 5 o'clock in the morning, the wounded officer breathing his last at 4:30 o'clock in the afternoon.[80]

Shortly after the murder, English had his wound dressed by his wife and his mother-in-law. Threatening to kill Burke, he left the house through the back door and made his escape. A coroner's jury was called, and English was found guilty of Wernith's death. His in-laws, Mr. and Mrs. A.J. Rummer, were also implicated.

The Elk County commissioners offered a reward of $1,000 for the arrest of English. The reward information described him as "35 years old; six feet high; heavy set; weight about 225 pounds; light hair and light complexion; usually wears a smooth face."[81]

When he left the area, English was well armed, and it was believed that he had a large number of friends who would provide provisions and alert him to potential discovery. Eventually, English reached the state of Michigan. Tiring of being a wanted man, he finally turned himself in.

The *Elk County Advocate* reported Harry English's appearance in court in Ridgway on September 30, 1880.

> *The case of the Commonwealth vs. Harry English was called at 9 o'clock. Deputy Sheriff Wensel brought the prisoner, Harry English, into court. He was neatly attired in a dark suit of clothes, hair trimmed and face smoothly shaven with shoes blackened. There was no appearance of bravado or daredevil demeanor, but instead a quiet, good looking young man came into court and took his place beside his counsel to be tried for the highest crime of which man can be charged. Viz: murder.*[82]

The trial lasted several days, with many witnesses called. There was some testimony having to do with the constables consuming a few drinks before they attempted to arrest Harry English for forgery. Other testimony implied that English acted as he did out of concern for his family, and that he acted in self-defense. There was testimony about who actually fired the shot from the gun that killed Wernith.

In the end, and with all the conflicting testimony, when the judge charged the jury, he questioned the authority of lawmen from another county to serve a warrant for arrest within Elk County. With little deliberation by the jury, Harry English was found not guilty. It was a popular decision among the audience, who rushed to his side to shake his hand and congratulate him.

But Harry English's troubles were not over. He was later convicted on a charge of forgery and fined $500 and served a term in the penitentiary. After his release, his health was broken, and he declined assistance from relatives, preferring to enter the McKean County Home, where he died in 1905.[83]

A SHOEMAKER CUTS THE THROAT OF ANOTHER
MAN'S WIFE, CONFESSES THE DEED
AND THEN CUTS HIS OWN THROAT

Newspapers in Pennsylvania reported a tragedy that occurred in Caledonia on June 24, 1876. Dolson Hicks was a shoemaker who had been in Caledonia for three years, boarding with a family named Shopland. About a year and a half earlier, Mr. Shopland died, leaving a four-year-old boy and a thirty-year-old widow, Phebe Shopland. Hicks continued to board with her.

Hicks, prosperous in business, had accumulated considerable property. While he was respected by those in the community, he was addicted to periodic spells of drinking. Phebe was left poor after her husband's death, and six months after he passed, she accepted an offer of marriage from Hicks on one condition: that he quit his periodic bouts of drinking. She gave him a year to prove himself.[84]

Shortly after Shopland's death, a young blacksmith, William Cochran, came to Caledonia to work in Smith's blacksmith shop. Cochran also found a boarding place with Phebe Shopland. When Cochran took up residence at the boardinghouse, Hicks became jealous of him. During a conversation between Hicks and Phebe Shopland, she noted that she considered Cochran a fine man. Hicks, angered by her words, went off on a drinking spree, which led to the widow breaking their engagement. Ten days later, she and the blacksmith, Cochran, were married.

In those ten days, Hicks, who had been passionate in his love for Phebe, began to drink more than he had before. Leaving his shop in the hands of a man who was working for him, Hicks sharpened a long-bladed knife, noting that he was going to trim some bushes for another lady in town and would be back later that afternoon. Around three o'clock in the afternoon, Hicks entered the blacksmith shop where Cochran was working with a bloodied knife in his hands and said, "You are a widower and I am a murderer." Cochran exclaimed, "He's murdered my wife!"[85]

Racing out of the shop to the house, Cochran found his wife, Phebe, on the floor with the little boy, weeping, lying on her. While there were no signs of a struggle, there were blood marks in two or three places around the room. Sending for the doctor, Cochran and others from the blacksmith shop started after Hicks. They found him in the shop. Cochran grabbed a sledgehammer and would have crushed Hicks to death if not for the interference of others there. Hicks begged them to let Cochran kill him as he wanted to die.

Hicks admitted to the murder.

He said he and the deceased had been engaged to be married for several months and she had failed to keep her promise. The fact that he was to have married Mrs. Shopland was well known and since she had jilted him he had been ridiculed and troubled with it. This so annoyed and enraged him that he determined to take her life. Four times before the fatal day he had started on his murderous errand, but always backed out. When he left his shop in the afternoon he went directly to the residence of the deceased. He said her little boy on the steps told him his mother was in. Hicks went in and found Mrs. Cochran sewing. She arose when he entered and told him to take a chair. He walked up to her and said, "Phebe, you have made a madman of me." She replied that she was sorry if she had injured him, but that he was as much to blame as herself. He then drew the knife from his pocket. She stepped back a step, but before she could make an outcry, he threw one arm around her and held her while he drew the knife across her throat four times, when she fell to the floor.[86]

At the inquest, Hicks pronounced all the testimony correct. He was then escorted to an area where he was to prepare to be taken to jail, thirty miles away. While two officers were watching over him, one had to leave the room to make arrangements to transport the prisoner. While his back was turned, the other guard heard a noise and turned to see the prisoner on his knees with his head on a bed and blood gushing from a wound in his throat. Hicks had cut his right carotid artery. Before the officer could reach him, Hicks cut another wound into his neck. The wounds were made with a large pocketknife with a four-inch blade. He died in a few minutes.[87]

Medix Run

Leonard Morey is credited with being the first settler in the Medix Run area around 1812; however, there may have been temporary settlements near the mouth of what was then known as Meddox Run before Morey arrived. History records that people by the name of Meddocs arrived in the area, staying for about a year on their way to Venango County.[88] A review of early census records did not reveal the name Meddocs in the area that became Elk County or in Venango County, but the history of people with the surname Meddocs who stayed for a short time in the region may provide an explanation for the name Medix, which may have been a colloquial version of Meddocs.

The village was the location of the first school in Elk County, which operated for 110 years, from 1821 until 1931.[89] The village did not grow after the school was opened, as one might expect, and a map dated 1871 gives evidence of the village of nearby Rock Hill but not of Medix Run.

Medix Run had its most rapid growth during its lumber days, when in 1893 the Medix Run Lumber Company erected a mill that included a boiler house with a stack of wrought iron extending 119 feet into the air, an engine room, a planing mill, a machine shop, a supply store, a business office and its own railroad. It employed about seventy-five men and could produce 110,000 feet of lumber a day. The Bennetts Branch Shingle Company operated at that same location.[90]

Taking advantage of all the hemlock growing in the area, the Gleason Tannery was located not far from the lumber mill and had a contract to take all the hemlock bark available from the mill to be used in its tanning business. It employed about forty-five people. Scanning the village today, it's hard to imagine the amount of industry that was there in an earlier time.

Graveyard of the Alleghenies

The steep hills surrounding the villages in the Benezette region required skillful pilots in the early days of aviation, with the area earning a reputation as the "Graveyard of the Alleghenies."

One pilot, Harry Smith, cheated the graveyard on a trip carrying mail from Cleveland to New York City. Smith related that the weather was cold but clear that January in 1928. On a night flight, at a time when there was no radio or radar for pilots to rely on, Smith followed a string of flashing beacon lights as he made his way to Bellefonte, where he was to refuel.

I was right on course when I passed the Murray Summit beacon west of Reynoldsville and the lights of DuBois were next. Then the McCall Hill beacon at Salem. I was watching for the beacon at Greenwood airport but some heavy snow squalls came up and I missed it. Next beacon would be Kylertown. At that time my engine started to set up and I knew I was in trouble. By great luck I ran out of the snow squalls and when I did, I was right over the Munn Farm [near Medix Run], I knew it right away as all pilots had the large field marked as a potential for emergency landings. I still had altitude enough to circle and drop a parachute flare to see which way the wind was blowing and came in for a safe landing just as the engine died.[91]

As he circled, Smith noted a building and, after landing, walked about a quarter of a mile to a hunting camp. As many camps were unlocked in those years, he made his way inside, where he found matches, kerosene lamps and dry wood. Making a fire and finding blankets, he was able to keep himself comfortable despite the extreme cold outside. He noted that there was coffee, tea, sugar, biscuits and butter, and he made a lunch.

Starting out at daybreak the next day in fresh snow, Smith took a wrong turn that led to a fourteen-mile hike to Medix Run. It was New Year's Day.

Imagine the surprise of two men from Falls Creek who were in the area running a trap line up Medix Run when they saw this figure coming toward them, dressed in a black leather fur-lined flying suit and helmet. Smith told them about his accident and said he needed to get to a telephone as soon as possible to report that the mail and the plane were safe. The trappers took Smith to their camp, giving him a pair of boots for his journey, and passed him off to a farm family around four o'clock in the afternoon, where Smith received additional assistance. Smith called the Cleveland Airport, where they were relieved to hear from him, as there had been no word about him

Douglas M2 mailplane. *FlugKerz2, Wikimedia Commons.*

after he passed Clarion. While Smith wanted to attempt to fly the plane out, his instructions were to secure the mail and get it to the Harrisburg airport.

The next day, Smith went back to the crash site to retrieve the mail, and when the passenger train from Red Bank to Driftwood stopped at Medix Run at eight o'clock that evening, Harry Smith and the mailbags were loaded on board for a trip to Harrisburg.

Getting the plane out of its landing place took great skill. It was a Douglas biplane with a water-cooled Liberty engine, and a new engine would have to be installed. A pilot and mechanic came in from Cleveland with equipment for the recovery effort. Making the plane as light as possible for takeoff and installing a new engine, they backed the plane up to a tree and tied a skid to it. When the pilot started the engine, the rope was cut and the plane went off like a big bird. The rescue pilot landed safely in Bellefonte, where he fueled up for the return trip to Cleveland.[92]

A Ghost Story

A popular spot in Medix Run is the Medix Hotel. According to its owner, it has a long history, as it was built in 1896. The hotel started out as a boardinghouse for the many loggers in the area around the turn of the twentieth century. It is described as follows: "Seven charming guest rooms, coffee bar, wi-fi, A/C, ATM. President Garfield and Roosevelt

Medix Hotel, Medix Run. *John Myers.*

slept here. Good food, outdoor seating, music, events, dubbed 'funniest bar in Benezette.'"[93]

Its owner claims that the hotel today is "home" to four guests from that bygone era: a man in the attic; Victoria, a woman who visits the downstairs bar; and a happy mother and child in room no. 7. In other words, spirits.

The staff and guests have experienced unexplainable events, such as pictures being removed from the walls and placed on the floor and bedspreads being removed, the explanation being that the "ghosts didn't like them."[94] The "presence" in the hotel has been sensed not only by staff but also by guests. The owner claims that the spirits seem to be protecting the hotel from damage, and she cites a specific time when she was awakened during the night "by some unseen entity" warning her about a burst pipe on the other side of the hotel. The spirit, Victoria, that likes to spend time in the bar is described as having white hair and wearing a "white, Victorian style dress."[95]

Mt. Pleasant/Winslow Hill

Farm Life

Mt. Pleasant or Winslow Hill? Today, certainly, Winslow Hill is the recognized name for this region just outside the Village of Benezette. But in an earlier time, this area had its own school, a church and approximately one hundred families living there and was known as Mt. Pleasant. It was a farming area, and the names of its residents are familiar in the region today: Winslow, Overturf, Jordan, Johnson, Rothrock, Mowrey and Woodring.[96]

In fact, farming was such a big part of community life that the Mt. Pleasant Grange was formed on December 3, 1889. It was accepted into the Pennsylvania State Grange on January 1, 1890. Organized by W.H. Meredith, it had fourteen charter members. It was officially registered as Mt. Pleasant Grange, No. 894, Patrons of Husbandry.[97] The Grange is "a fraternal family organization dedicated to the betterment of the American way of life through community service, education, legislation and fellowship....It is the oldest agricultural and rural advocacy organization of its kind in the United States."[98]

An object that came into the hands of the youngest grandchild of Eva Winslow sheds some light on one aspect of farm life: the traveling salesman.

Eva Winslow was born in 1875 and grew up in the house built by her father, William K. Winslow, which is still standing at the bottom of Dewey

Road just below the Winslow Hill Elk Viewing Area. In 1887, when she was twelve years old, she made a trip to DuBois, Clearfield County, which is approximately thirty miles from Benezette. Most likely Eva, along with her parents, traveled by train. While in DuBois, Eva purchased a Galaxy Album—in today's terminology, an autograph book. The book is filled with signatures and verses from her friends and family, offering a nostalgic look at a bygone era before Twitter, Facebook and text messages.

Eva Winslow died in 1967, and some years later, the little album came into the hands of her grandchild. One page, however, was a mystery—a page filled with strange ciphers, possibly some form of shorthand. Family members speculated over the meaning of the "writing," even holding the page up to mirrors to see if it could be read backward or upside down. It wasn't until 2019, when a photo of the page in question was shared with members of a literary group, that someone suggested the "ciphers" might be Yiddish. Eva's grandchild reached out to a teacher of Jewish Studies at the University of Pittsburgh, who confirmed that indeed the strange marks on the paper were Yiddish; however, translating it was beyond the teacher's skill level. Eventually, a Yiddish-to-English translator was located and, for the most part, was able to translate the message. The dots represent places where the ciphers were beyond the translator's ability to recognize the words.

Mt. Pleasant Grange ribbon. The National Grange of the Order of Patrons of Husbandry is a U.S. social organization founded in 1867 after the Civil War to promote the well-being of communities and agriculture. *Kathy Myers.*

Miss Evy Winslow, the one who understands when I come to see her in her place, the beauty that shines and the consolation that…when I come in the house and I…and I thought that she is just delightful. Her hair is black and her eyes are blue and I am very glad that I had the pleasure to talk to her. When I look through the window, the…Jews that…and I am glad that I have the pleasure to write in her album, to write a dedication, but what to write and what to do, and I am glad that I had the chance to be acquainted with you, your true friend.[99]

Beard & Johnson, *Winslow* Du Bois Pa,

Twelve-year-old
Eva Winslow, with
her long dark hair
and blue eyes.
Kathy Myers.

Her "true friend" was a traveling salesman passing through the farming region calling on customers—apparently a regular, as he knew Eva well enough to refer to her as Evy. The message does not reveal the traveling salesman's name or who he worked for, but according to the translator, he wrote in German Yiddish.

The Winslow home also contained a piece of furniture that was sold through a mail-order catalog, an oak Chautauqua desk manufactured by the Larkin Soap Company. The Larkin Soap Company was founded in 1875 in Buffalo, New York, by John D. Larkin. He started selling soap through door-to-door sales to residential customers in 1881. His first product was a yellow

Left, top: Autograph book purchased in DuBois, Pennsylvania, 1887. *Kathy Myers.*

Left, bottom: Yiddish writing in the autograph book. *Kathy Myers.*

Opposite: The Chautauqua desk. *Larkin Company 1905 Premium List, Buffalo, New York.*

laundry bar named Sweet Home Soap. In its early days, the Larkin Company, expanding its product line, developed the idea of inserting a premium into every box of soap, the first such premium being a picture of the company's logo. Eventually, handkerchiefs were included with the "Pure White" toilet soap and then a bath towel with the purchase of "Ocean Bath" soap. As the company grew, it was able to offer better premiums.[100] Eventually, Larkin began selling his products through mail-order only, and by 1906, the Larkin catalogue contained hundreds of items. The Chautauqua desk owned by the Winslow family was one of Larkin's most popular giveaways. For a ten-dollar order of soap, the customer would receive both the soap and the desk as a premium. "The Chautauqua desk is the most recognized piece of furniture offered in the 1901 Larkin catalogue."[101]

The Famous Chautauqua Desk No. 5.

Given for five Certificates; or free with $10.00 worth of Larkin Soaps and Products.

This beautiful Desk is made of solid Oak, hand-polished Golden Oak finish; very handsome carvings. Drop-leaf provides a writing-bed 26 in. deep, 29½ in. high. Fine 8 x 14 in. French beveled-plate mirror; brass rod for curtains. It stands 5 ft. high, is 2½ ft. wide and 10½ in. deep.

It is a perfect and complete but remarkably compact Desk, and also has three roomy book-shelves, two shelves for bric-a-brac; seven pigeon-holes for papers, compartments for letter-paper, ink, etc., under lock and key.

Roll-Top Oak Desk No. 913.

Given for thirteen Certificates. With Soaps, see page 3. "Built-up" bed, Golden Oak finish. Size, 42 in. long, 30 in. wide, 47 in. high. Two keys to lock; eight pigeon-holes, 2¾ x 4 in. Two stationery compartments, 1¼ in. high; 12½ in. wide; two ledger compartments 2 x 14 in.; all 9 in. deep. Two small drawers, 2 x 6½ x 7½ in.; pencil and blotter rack.

In the pedestal there are three roomy drawers 20½ in. long, 11 in. wide and 3½, 4½ and 11½ in. deep, respectively, which lock automatically when top is closed. Weight, 175 lbs.

School

A search of the records does not reveal the date that the Mt. Pleasant School for elementary students was established. It was in service until 1931, when it was closed and students were taken to Benezette.[102] The building is now used as a hunting camp.

A news article dated June 29, 1881, titled "Our Schools" provides some information about the school, which was in operation at least fifty years.

> *The Mount Pleasant school is under the guidance of Miss Jennie Hyman and is attended by about twenty-five pupils. Some of the pupils by sickness and other causes have been kept absent for awhile, but the attendance now is good. The apparatus is ample and the school house is in excellent condition.*[103]

Victoria Winslow, born in 1903, was one of the students at that school. The daughter of Edward and Walburga Winslow, she grew up in the house built by her father's uncle, George Winslow. George Winslow, according to Winslow family tradition, is said to have named Winslow Hill.

A tablet from Victoria's school days, written in her own hand, cursive style, provides an interesting look at the teaching of history in local schools at that time. Beginning with "George Washington, Federalist," the tablet details the history of the United States through the administration of "Theodore Roosevelt, Republican," ending in 1909. In a general summary of the history lessons learned over a period of time, Victoria wrote,

> *Birth of Republic—It started from a few feeble colonies at first, development of common wealth. The people—We take census every year. We find that we have grown very much and we can get free education here, even the foreign people. We have strong armies and strong navies. Our motto is* AMERICA MEANS OPPORTUNITY.[104]

Victoria's brothers and sister, James, Lawrence, Theodore and Agnes, attended school at Mt. Pleasant as well.

Artist's rendition of 1852 home built by George Winslow, taken down in preparation for Winslow Hill Elk Viewing Area. *Winslow House Heritage Council.*

Winslow Hill Viewing Area. *John Myers.*

The home where the Winslow children grew up passed through the family to Victoria's brother Lawrence and finally to his daughter Betty Gilbert and her husband, Ken. The house, which was built between 1850 and 1860, and two hundred acres of land were eventually purchased from the Gilberts by the Western Pennsylvania Conservancy and donated to the Commonwealth of Pennsylvania for the use of the Game Commission. While the Game Commission was involved in mine recovery activities in that location prior to establishing the viewing area, in an unprecedented move, it consented to give the house to Winslow House Heritage Council, a local nonprofit, with the provision it be moved from the land. Winslow House Heritage Council was incorporated in November 2004 for the purpose of preserving and promoting the history, natural resource heritage, wildlife resources and local lore of the Winslow Hill Region. Unfortunately, after completion of a feasibility study on moving the house funded by a grant from the commonwealth, the Heritage Council was unable to secure funding to purchase land to relocate the house. In the end, the house was taken down by the Game Commission, and the house site and its acreage became part of the Winslow Hill Elk Viewing Area.[105]

THE MT. PLEASANT METHODIST CHURCH
on Winslow Hill. The cornerstone
of this church was laid in 1896.
The structure is now a hunting lodge.

Top: Mt. Pleasant Methodist Church. *Elk County Historical Society.*

Bottom: Former Mt. Pleasant Church, now a hunting camp. *John Myers.*

Church

The Mt. Pleasant Methodist Church was one of four original sites for a church when the Caledonia circuit was established in 1858. Prior to that time, services were provided by the Ridgway Circuit and held in the log cabins of the early settlers. The physical building at Mt. Pleasant was erected in 1896, as evidenced by its cornerstone, and had an active congregation until 1947, when the worshippers were shifted to the Benezette Methodist Church.[106] The church was converted to a hunting camp.

Day Turned Into Night

> *Birds went to roost and cattle moved in from fields as is in the evening. One youngster said, "Gramp, give me enough money to see the show—it may be the last one I'll see."*[107]

Merton Winslow (known as Mert) was born on Winslow Hill in 1888. He grew to manhood in the house built by his father located at the bottom of Dewey Road just below the Winslow Hill Elk Viewing Area. The youngest of the boys in his family, he spent his life on Winslow Hill.

Mert married Ada Johnson of Grant in 1916. Her ancestors were among the original settlers of Grant. Mert and Ada settled in a house just over the hill from his father's home. It was also very near the home of his grandparents Charles and Rebecca Hicks Winslow, built in 1845 and now in private ownership. Mert and Ada were typical farmers, growing crops, caring for their milk cows and eventually owning a large chicken farm, selling eggs to area grocery stores.

The happy couple raised two sons, Gerald and Thomas. Gerald returned home from World War II and initially settled in Buffalo, New York, while Tom was called by the military to a new battle.

In 1950, war had broken out on the Korean Peninsula, and the United States became embroiled in the conflict. It was the era of the Cold War with Russia. Throughout the region, signs were attached to sturdy buildings designating them shelters from nuclear attack. Children were taught to hide under their desks at school in case of attack. The draft was in effect, and young men were called into service.

On Sunday, September 24, 1950, Mert and Ada, absent their own sons, were entertaining Mert's sister, Eva, and her son, Winslow Smith, along with his wife and youngest child.

Sixteen-year-old Mert Winslow (*far right*) and family, sitting on the porch of his parents' homestead. *Kathy Myers.*

After enjoying a dinner of farm-raised roast chicken, topped off with an ice cream dessert, the group made its way to the side porch of the house, where they could look out across the fields to what Mert referred to as the round top, the hill where a fire tower stood.

About two o'clock in the afternoon on that sunny fall day, the family noticed the sky beginning to darken. Slowly, strange-looking clouds moved in over the round top, and the sunshine soon gave way to dusk. The chickens went to roost in their coop. Quickly, dusk gave way to total darkness.

This was a time without hundreds of radio or television stations or any means for instant updates. While electricity had been extended to Winslow Hill in 1948, there was no TV at the farmhouse, and the local radio station was at a loss to give an explanation of what was taking place.[108] Phone service was scarce, but the Winslows had a telephone, and while long-distance calls were infrequently made, given the unusual circumstances, Winslow Smith's wife called their home in Ridgway, where their three older children were that day.

Their oldest daughter answered the phone. It was so dark in town, she said, that the streetlights were lit. People were driving cars with the headlights on. She also noted that there appeared to be some panic. Neighbors had reportedly gone to church, believing that the end of the world was at hand. The radio in their home operated on an antenna that received stations from outside the region. Tuning into a Pittsburgh station, she noted it was reporting that the darkness was caused by wildfires raging in Canada, with the smoke moving over the Great Lakes and through the skies of northwest Pennsylvania.

On the fortieth anniversary of this anomaly, a local newspaper ran an article that recalled the event, describing it as "day being turned into night," when the sun was completely blocked out in the sky and an eerie darkness enveloped the community. The article pointed out that when people attended the Sunday matinee at the theater, they saw the sun was shining brightly, only to come out a couple of hours later into midnight darkness. As news began to circulate over leased wire services to local stations, tensions began to relax. The author of the news article also drew a contrast between the amount of instant information received today and the fact that most people then didn't have TV and the major source of information was the radio.[109]

The smoke had traveled approximately 1,500 miles. Locally, the darkness blended into nighttime, while areas in eastern Pennsylvania experienced the darkness for a couple of hours. One newspaper stated it was "an exact repetition of a blackout occurring in 1780 and repeated on a lesser scale at least a few times in the past century."[110]

Mert's chickens roosted until daybreak the next day, and the Smith family drove to their home in Ridgway around three o'clock in the afternoon in darkness.

Fast forward to June 2023. As a "haze" crept in over the Wilds region, the cause was noted as forest fires in Canada. Many news outlets appeared to have no knowledge of this 1950 event, reporting that this had never happened before. However, in the fall of 2008, a PhD student in the Department of Physics at the University of Toronto wrote an article, "Revisiting the 1950 Great Smoke Pall." He noted that after a dry summer in northern British Columbia and Alberta, there was an outbreak of fires in mid-September.

> *The biggest of these, the Chinchaga, burned between 3,500,000 and 4,200,000 acres of forest land making it possibly the biggest fire in North America's recorded history.... The smoke disrupted aircraft flights over much*

of Ontario, with pilots from Sault Ste. Marie to London flying through midnight-like conditions in the brown cloud....From Ontario the smoke continued into Ohio, New York and Pennsylvania. In fact, as it crossed the border, the lights on the Peace Bridge from Ft. Erie, Ontario to Buffalo, NY, had to be turned on as did stadium lights for afternoon baseball games in Cleveland, Pittsburgh and New York City....In Watts Flatts, NY, Mrs. Dora Gesaman announced gravely that at 4 p.m. when the overcast lifted, her rooster crowed as if it were dawn and the chickens left the roost under the impression day had arrived.[111]

The smoke was noticed across western and southern Europe, not as a thick brown cloud but as a blue sun during the day and a blue moon at night, with reports coming from as far east as Poland and as far south as Malta.[112] What the Winslow family members experienced on Winslow Hill that September day in 1950 was more severe than the 2023 Canadian fire season.

SUMMERSON

Dr. Daniel Rogers, mentioned in an earlier chapter, began clearing an area for his home in what is now Summerson in 1812. Early settlers such as Andrew Overturf, Amos Mix, Thomas Dent and Ralph Johnson were all early callers.

The village was named for Mrs. Summerson, an early settler at Sterling Run in Cameron County. The Buffalo and Susquehanna Railroad Station there was named Greene, with the station shelter located across the Bennett's Branch from the Village of Summerson, approximately halfway between Benezette and Dents Run. A siding and loading docks were present there about 1917. The Pennsylvania Railroad maintained a station across from Summerson that was called Mt. Pleasant Station.[113]

From 1897 to 1902, logs were floated from Summerson down the Bennett's Branch to Williamsport. A logging railroad of four miles was built, with a sawmill running from 1912 to 1915. Over the years, other industries have included a large chicken farm and a feed and flour mill.[114]

GRANT

Ulysses S. Grant, circa 1870–1880. *Wikimedia Commons.*

In 1812, Ralph and Rebecca (Brooks) Johnson, natives of Yorkshire, England, came to the Benezette region and settled in what is today known as Grant. They cleared a farm and engaged in lumbering, and in 1830, Ralph Johnson built a sawmill. Ralph and Rebecca reared a family of thirteen children.[115]

The town was then known as Dry Sawmill, and the greatest number of its homes were built around 1870, with its main industry, sawmills, being the attraction. In 1868, Cornelius Wainright erected a sawmill, which was followed by a water-powered sawmill in 1870 built by Ralph Johnson. Sawmills were erected in 1895 and 1900, with another mill operating as late as 1948 to 1950.[116] Sometime after a visit by President Grant, the name of the village was permanently changed to Grant.

President Grant seems to have had a special interest in the area known today as the Wilds. He is known to have visited Elk County on three different occasions; his visit to Dry Sawmill, his second trip into the Wilds, took place in 1873.[117]

Grant was not an imposing man, standing just five feet, eight and a half inches tall, but he had a somewhat rugged appearance, with a heavy beard and a cigar either in his mouth or in his hand. He was known to drink a substantial amount of whiskey, and he liked to ride fast horses. But he was also seen as a good family man, parenting four children at the White House.[118] On his first trip to Elk County, his son Jesse accompanied him. On his second trip, which was to Dry Sawmill, he was accompanied by government notables.

Apparently, the trip was refreshing for the president, as it was reported, "There is no doubt that the President enjoyed his short vacation in Bennett's Valley and that upon his return to Washington he felt better able to cope with the tremendous responsibilities of the presidency."[119]

The *Elk County Advocate* published an article that features a local's observations of the visit.

Jay, June 2nd, 1873

Dear Advocate—Our vicinity has been visited by distinguished excursionists, which of course, has been the subject of much comment among the natives. Last week President Grant, the Postmaster General, Secretary of State, Don Cameron, Calvin Naree and other distinguished gentlemen spent two days along our streams, trout fishing, etc., and to all appearances they enjoyed themselves hugely. It has been suggested (probably by a Democrat) that Bourbon suffered more than the trout. We are told the party were not experts at angling, but fishermen's wages took a sudden raise and for two days run up to eight dollars with an upward tendency at the close of the first day. One man fished all day and reported at evening with four trout and got for his services, eight dollars in cash and a good appetite.[120]

From this account, it appears that the "distinguished excursionists" were not very good fishermen and were paying the locals to bring in their daily catch for the evening meal. The article goes on to report about the group's "itch for venison."

There was rather a good joke got off on the party by two citizens somewhat noted as hunters, who, for short we will call Carp & Sol. They applied to Carp & Sol for a deer and were told that it was out of the season, it would take fifty dollars to pay the fine and venison would be "dear" meat. But who cares for expenses; they must have a deer killed before they left. Carp is rather fruitful and suggested to Colonel Philips (President of the Allegheny Valley Road) who had the party in charge, that he knew of just one chance for a deer, and if he would steam up and run them up the line a ways they would try it. They ran up opposite Jake English's and Carp & Sol crossed over to negotiate for a tame deer. Jake would sell the deer for fifty dollars, but the old buck was so poor that Carp and Sol returned without him. Philips said poor or not they must have the deer. So Carp and Sol killed and dressed the deer. Philips paid Jake $50s and returned to the Presidential party. Who, supposing it to be a wild deer right from his forest home, gave Carp and Sol twenty dollars for their hunting exploits and left in fine spirits for Washington with Jake English's old buck.

We can appreciate the visits of President Grant and his attendants to Elk County as highly as anyone, but consider an open violation of the Laws of Pennsylvania as reprehensible in a President as in a private citizen.[121]

DENTS RUN

Dents Run was settled by Thomas and Elizabeth Dent, natives of England, who were among the first settlers of Elk and Cameron Counties.

By 1845, the village had its greatest growth, with a population of 185 people. The lumber industry provided most of the employment, while some additional employment was found in the mines at Wilmer.[122]

In 1881, Miles Dent, one of the leading lumbermen in Pennsylvania, erected a sawmill; in 1883–85, he constructed a railroad bridge; and in 1888, he erected a store. W.A. Hatton was the owner of a popular hotel, which was destroyed by fire in 1889. Little is left of the village's boom years. The last large sawmill closed in 1906, and railroad service was eventually terminated.[123]

But Dents Run has gained national attention recently due to the recurring story of a lost Civil War gold shipment. The legend is told in Alice Wessman's *A History of Elk County, Pennsylvania 1981* of a missing Civil War gold shipment that has intrigued treasure hunters for over a hundred years and, as recently as 2018, was the subject of an actual search in Elk County by the FBI and the Department of Conservation and Natural Resources.

Under the heading "Thar's Gold in Them Thar Hills?" the historian relates a tale of a gold shipment arriving outside of Ridgway, the county seat, in June 1863, when a caravan of wagons and armed horsemen made their way up a Clarion River trail to a clearing, where they rested for the night. The caravan was made up of two heavy canvas-covered freight wagons and one of the smaller covered wagons known to the army as ambulances. There were four mules, three drivers and eight men on horseback. According to the historian, "Concealed beneath false bottoms of the large wagons were twenty-six black painted ingots or bars of partly refined gold, each weighing fifty pounds and worth about $10,000 each."[124] Supposedly, the gold was being transported from Pittsburgh to Philadelphia, where it was intended for the Federal Mint. Because of concerns about guerrilla attacks on railroads in southern Pennsylvania, a secret route through Elk County had been devised.

Gold ingots. *Wikimedia Commons.*

The main characters in this story were the caravan's commander, Lieutenant Castleton; Sergeant Mike O'Rourke; and another man only identified as Connors. The names of the others in the caravan were not revealed.

Castleton was said to have been born into a famous military family; however, his combat career was ended by a hip wound, and he suffered from malaria. O'Rourke was "rough and tough and wanted by the police for several murderous river port brawls....He possessed a natural talent for leadership and shrewdness that Castleton lacked."[125] Connors was just plain "sullen, mean and unfriendly and had been wounded in combat."[126]

Castleton and O'Rourke, riding together into Ridgway, found they were not welcome. Visiting a tavern, the two men were accused of being recruiters and drafters (the draft was not popular). A fight broke out, and the two escaped. The next day, wisely detouring around Ridgway, the caravan set off for St. Marys, along what is today's State Route 120, arriving two days later.

Once in St. Marys, they located a map made in 1842 by a survey crew of what was described as Wild Cat Country showing a possible road branching off about ten miles east of St. Marys, going over the mountains and following a stream to the Sinnemahoning Creek. Deciding to follow this route, the caravan apparently made some wrong turns and became lost.

Castleton was weak from fever, and the rest of the party was exhausted. After some discussion, it was decided that Connors would take two men and start out on foot southeast toward the village of Sinnemahoning to get help. Castleton and the five other men would transfer the gold from the wagons to the pack mules' saddles, and the men and mules would travel south. Before Connors left, Castleton gave him a written report summarizing the journey to that point and "a Federal Army order authorizing Connors to requisition men and supplies for the party's aid."[127] Connors later reported that when he left, Castleton and O'Rourke were arguing about whether they should transport all the gold on the mules or bury part of it.

Connors returned ten days later with a rescue party from Lock Haven; however, all they found were the abandoned wagons. It appeared the main party had split up. After searching for several days, the rescuers returned to Lock Haven without the lost men or the gold.

The War Department in Washington was notified, and a court of inquiry was held in Clearfield, charging Castleton and O'Rourke with treason and theft. However, due to the status of Castleton's military family, charges were suspended pending investigation.

The Pinkerton Agency, being the main source of army intelligence at that time, was given the assignment of locating the lost gold and the men who had disappeared. Working in secrecy, the Pinkerton men took on the personas of prospectors or lumbermen to avoid detection by the locals as they searched the Bennett's Branch of the Sinnemahoning Creek as far west as St. Marys.[128]

What they found in 1865 was scarce evidence: two and a half gold ingots buried under a pine stump about four miles from the spot where the wagons had been abandoned. To the experienced detectives, this indicated theft and a division of the gold.

In 1866, other Pinkerton detectives located one of the army mules. The mule, which carried the army brand, was found, according to the man in possession at the time, wandering in the woods.[129]

In 1876, when the Elk-Cameron County boundary line was resurveyed, surveyors found the bones of three to five skeletons near a springhead near Dents Run, about seven miles from where the wagons had been abandoned.

Fast-forward to 2018. Finders Keepers, a local lost treasure recovery service, maintains that it found the lost gold shipment in an area of Dents Run Road in 2012 and that federal law kept them from digging for it. In March of 2018, the *DuBois Courier-Express* carried a story about the treasure, along with a photo of where FBI agents set up to search for the gold. The *Courier* also reported that an FBI spokeswoman on-site "said agents were conducting court authorized law enforcement activity."[130]

The FBI claimed it found nothing. The treasure hunters are asking for proof. Finders Keepers recovery services hired an attorney to obtain the results of the FBI search in the area where Finders Keepers believes the lost gold was found. The attorney claims the FBI has dragged its feet on the treasure hunters' Freedom of Information Act request for records. "The FBI initially claimed it had no files about the investigation. Then, after the Justice Department ordered a more thorough review, the FBI said its records were exempt from public disclosure. Finally, in the wake of the treasure hunters' appeal, the FBI said it had located 2,300 pages of records and 17 video files that it could potentially turn over—but that it would take years to do so."[131]

On June 5, 2022, a local television station reported that a federal judge ordered the FBI to speed up the release of records. According to the report, "The FBI must turn over one thousand pages of records per month, starting in thirty days, and the first batch of records must include a key report sought by Finders Keepers, U.S. District Judge Amit P. Metah ordered."[132] As of the writing of this book, no further evidence has been forthcoming.

However, on October 8, 2023, another news story appeared, titled "Witnesses to FBI Hunt in Elk County for Civil War Gold Describe What They Saw." The article, published by WTAJ, records the recollections of two men, Eric McCarthy and his client, Don Reichel, in the Dents Run area who were up before sunrise to look for "sheds," freshly shed elk antlers, to add to Reichel's collection. At the same time, a team of FBI agents was hunting for the lost gold. McCarthy, an elk guide, said he had never met the treasure hunters or anybody involved in the gold recovery project, explaining that after reading news accounts, he felt he needed to say what he saw.[133]

McCarthy recalled that the FBI had shooed him away from a different part of Dents Run a day earlier. Determined to find some elk sheds, the men awoke at four o'clock in the morning and were at the site they chose between five and five thirty. McCarthy dropped Reichel off and parked approximately a mile away. As he exited the truck, McCarthy could hear the sound of a running engine off in the distance. He described the sound he heard as he made his way up the hill as metal on stone or metal on metal—in other words, heavy equipment meeting earth. Once he got to the top of the hill and started down the other side, he saw lights powered by a generator and several pieces of equipment moving up and down the hill. He noted there was a brown-black gash in the earth surrounded by snow. Reichel also heard the clanging of equipment as he climbed the ridge but was too far away to see anything.[134]

The FBI's warrant to conduct the search limited work to between the hours of 6:00 a.m. and 10:00 p.m. each day. The FBI denies any after-hours digging and says it conducted patrols by ATV at nighttime to secure the site. It claims that on the morning in question, the FBI search team didn't arrive at the site until 8:00 a.m., well past the time that McCarthy and Reichel were in the area.[135]

When McCarthy and Reichel met for lunch several hours later, they witnessed a convoy of unmarked black SUVs and armored trucks driving by on Route 555, leaving Dents Run. Both men reported that one of the three armored trucks was weighed down, noting, "That one must be loaded."[136]

The owner of Finders Keepers and his attorney met with officials from the Pennsylvania Department of Conservation and Natural Resources in late October 2023 to seek the agency's assistance. On September 27, 2023, Judge Amit Mehta refuted the FBI's assertion that it is exempt from disclosing its operational plan for the gold dig, stating that the agency needs to come up with better justification for keeping its records under wraps.[137]

HICKS RUN

The site of Hicks Run village was located along the boundary line between Elk and Cameron and is today known for its elk-viewing opportunities. According to the Pennsylvania Game Commission:

> *Hicks Run Viewing Area is adjacent to the Hicks Run Cemetery along Route 555 on the Elk State Forest. This viewing area with blind, overlooks high-quality elk forage. Elk are commonly present there early and late in the day all year. It's a great stop to tie into a fall foliage ride and the viewing blind offers fine photography opportunities. The viewing area is along Route 555 about 12 miles east of Benezette, near Hicks Run Road. Off-highway parking is available. Please park with care and be respectful of the cemetery.*[138]

The Hicks Run Cemetery is the resting place for many of the village's early settlers. In 1806, Levi Hicks, along with Andrew Overturf and Samuel Smith, came into the region. Hicks settled between First Fork and Second Fork (First Fork being Sinnemahoning and Second Ford being Driftwood), where he cleared about thirty acres of land. In 1812, he sold the land and

Hicks Run Wildlife Viewing Area. *John Myers.*

This page: Hicks Run Wildlife Viewing Area. *John Myers.*

Worn tombstones of John and Mary Elizabeth Conway Hicks, Hicks Run Cemetery.
John Myers.

moved up the Bennett's Branch to the mouth of Hicks Run. The property
was owned by his descendants for many years.[139] While it would appear
that the Hicks name that attached itself to the village and the run was that
of Levi Hicks, one historian, John Meginness, publisher of the *Journal of
Samuel Maclay*, notes that Hicks Run was named for Gershom Hicks, who
was known as a "White Indian," as mentioned in an earlier chapter.[140]

Traveling along Route 555 today, one cannot fathom what Hicks Run
once was: a thriving lumbering community with "ninety homes, a row built
northward across the road from a board-yard, and another eastward up the
mountain side along the edge of the woods."[141] Most were tenant houses.
One street was named Church Street—though ironically, there was never a
church at Hicks Run but rather a schoolhouse that was utilized for church
services. It stood on a hill very near the cemetery.[142] The community was able
to support the Hicks Run store, which sold iron beds, mattresses, springs,
blankets, axes, shoes and underwear.[143]

Site of the former village of Hicks Run, now an elk viewing area, *John Myers.*

From 1904 to 1912, Hicks Run flourished due to the business acumen of John E. DuBois—nephew and heir of John DuBois Jr., founder of the city of DuBois—and others who were involved in railroading and lumbering. By 1906, Hicks Run Mill, established in 1905, had begun to operate night and day with a double shift. This resulted in cutting almost in half the lifespan of the Hicks Run operation, which was estimated to run through 1918; production ended there by 1912. It was reported that when the last logs went through the Hicks Run Mill, it had produced 280 million board feet of timber.[144] The workers packed up and left for other jobs, many finding employment in other lines of work in DuBois.

But what happened to all the houses? One report is that a Reverend Beal purchased the better homes and moved them to DuBois. Another narrative, according to the two daughters of John Hicks, was that their father permitted his farm to be used as a site for the town, saying he had been given verbal assurance that he was promised the houses. In the end, with the majority of the houses moved to DuBois, the family received only three houses that had little value.[145]

Today, most of the land is either state game lands or part of the Elk State Forest.

MIX RUN

Conducting a Google search for "Mix Run" reveals that it is "an unincorporated village located in Gibson Township, Cameron County. The village is not tracked by the U.S. Census Bureau." What this suggests is that any residents in the area are counted as part of another nearby village.

Amos Mix and his wife were early settlers, coming into the region in 1812.[146] As with other villages in the region, the early lumber industry was important to Mix Run's inhabitants. But the village became well known for another reason: it was the birthplace of a famous Hollywood cowboy of early films, Thomas Hezekiah Mix—or to his fans, Tom Mix.

Through his maternal line, Tom was the great-great-grandson of John Barr, a soldier in the Revolutionary War who was born in County Mayo, Ireland, and immigrated to the United States. In February 1777, Barr enlisted in the Continental army, in a group known as Hartley's Regiment, in Delaware. He served in the military for three years and eleven months, participating in the Battles of Springfield, Brandywine, Germantown, Morristown and Paoli.[147]

Life was simple for young Tom in those early years. His father, Edwin, was an accomplished horseman who managed, trained and drove horses for a living. In 1888, Edwin moved the family to DuBois, where he became employed by lumberman John E. DuBois, managing his stock and stables. Edwin also taught his young son as much as he could about horsemanship. Tom, whose formal education ended when he finished grade school, was an apprentice into his teens.

On April 21, 1898, when Tom was eighteen, the Spanish-American War broke out, and Tom enlisted in the army on April 26. His military record indicates that he enlisted as Thomas Edwin Mix, using his father's name for his middle name; his occupation was "laborer"; he had brown eyes, black hair and dark complexion; and he was five feet, ten inches tall. By 1901, he had risen to the rank of first sergeant. He reenlisted in 1901, but by October 25, 1902, he was listed as a deserter, although he was never charged.[148] His Hollywood publicists greatly glorified his role in the military in later biographies. In reality, he went AWOL to marry his first wife.

Heading west to get a new start in life, he found work at a ranch in Oklahoma. The ranch owners ran a popular Wild West touring show, and with his fine skills as a horseman, he became a featured performer. Eventually, he became one of the greatest Wild West stars, along with his best-known horse, Tony. In contrast to his simple Mix Run/DuBois upbringing, Mix's

Left: Tom Mix (*left*) and his parents, Edwin and Elizabeth Hicks. *DuBois Area Historical Society.*

Below: Tom Mix. *Library of Congress.*

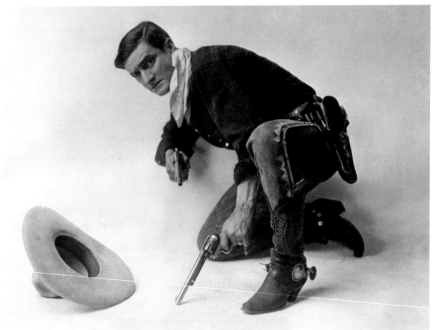

fame provided him with a lavish lifestyle. He died in an automobile crash near Florence, Arizona, in 1940.[149]

In 1986, the Mix Homestead was neglected and weed-choked, with a heap of rocks remaining that had once been part of the foundation. Ray Flaugh, a former U.S. Marine, and his wife, Eva, purchased the property and began a journey to assemble a collection of classic photos and artifacts to erect a museum. Money was raised by selling "lifetime memberships which entitled the bearer to a symbolic one-inch-square plot of the homestead. Ronald Reagan was one of the more than four thousand people who purchased memberships."[150]

With money raised, the Flaughs rebuilt the Mix house, an outhouse and a barn, turning the property into the Tom Mix Birthplace Park and Museum. For a time, the museum attracted a steady crowd. The Flaughs also sponsored a "Tom Mix Roundup" that featured mock shootouts and hangings, Western dress-up contests, country music and a Mix look-alike competition. Eventually, attendance declined, and the Flaughs closed the museum in 2002. The property was sold and turned into a campground.[151]

For several years, a Tom Mix Festival was held in the city of DuBois, where he once resided with his family.

CASTLE GARDEN

Why, in the middle of the Pennsylvania Wilds, would one come across a village with the name Castle Garden? "Castle Garden" conjures up images of gardens with flowers and hedges, castles—an elegant location. Actually, there was such a location in the early history of this country: Castle Garden, America's first official immigrant examining and processing center. From August 1, 1855, through April 18, 1890, immigrants arriving in the state of New York came through this processing center—approximately eight million of them, mostly from Germany, Ireland, England, Scotland, Sweden, Italy, Russia and Denmark.[152]

The history of Castle Garden, Pennsylvania, is tied in with that of its neighboring village, Driftwood. History reports that a large number of Irish immigrants into the region helped Driftwood achieve prosperity.[153]

A review of federal census records shed some light on Irish immigrants in Gibson Township, Cameron County, where Castle Garden is located. A sampling from 1850 and 1860 shows a smattering of Irish born in the area. The Potato Famine that caused massive migration out of Ireland was from 1845 to 1852, which may account for some of the Irish immigrants in Gibson Township.

However, the census of 1870 reveals a greater number of people than in the other two census years who listed their birthplace as Ireland. Many may have been recent immigrants starting off life in a new location, as many were married and in their twenties with no children or with young

Left: Bridge at Castle Garden, Pennsylvania, across the Bennett's Branch. *Library of Congress.*

Below: Gleason Tannery workmen at Driftwood, 1920. Many Irish names are listed. *Cameron County Historical Society.*

George McKimm, Sr., sent us our picture this week from Driftwood showing us the workmen and one Miss employed by the Gleason Tannery in that borough in 1920. The tannery was established in 1889 by L. R. Gleason and Son's and at that time promised to rival the great tanneries of the area. The works employed 35 men and produced a car-load of leather a week.
First row: Jess McKimm, Oscar Berry, George Morton, Ed McKimm, Tom Smith, Floyd Gemall, Pete Staff, Eddy Chase, Harry Callahan, Wallace Johnson, Eddy Eggler, Frank Eggler, Tippy Kreider, Ruth Wheeler, Olin Barr, Asa McKimm, Bert Russell, Charley Cooper, Dave, Wronk, Jimmy Charles.
Second row: Frank Mack, Frank Morton, Forrest Miller, John Eggler, Floyd Coleman, Charley Duell, Bill Callahan, Frank Miller, TommyMack, Fred Eggler, Fred Miller, Ed Eggler, Bill Genall, Bill Froman, Freeland Smith, Lonnie Arnold, Superintendent Ralph Whittaker, _____, _____. Allen, Albert Eggler, Bill Eggler.

children born in Pennsylvania. Others were older, in their forties, with a mixture of children born in Ireland and Pennsylvania, possibly having been in the United States longer. Some were living in individual homes, while others were living in boardinghouses or hotels. Most of them were laborers. The names were a mixture of familiar Irish names: Bolton, Lynch, Cashman, Sullivan, Martin, Mohney, Mullins, Murray, Kacey, Ford, Daly and O'Neil, among others.

History records that the Irish were not warmly welcomed by longtime citizens, so these people looked for locations to settle near Driftwood, one being Goosetown, where the community raised geese to furnish meat and feathers for bedding. The other, Castle Garden, was named for the familiar federal immigration station in New York City through which they passed.[154]

DRIFTWOOD

Driftwood is known in the region as the jumping-off place for the famous Bucktail Regiment of the Civil War, which began its journey to Harrisburg in support of the war effort on wooden rafts built nearby and floated into Sinnemahoning Creek (that history is detailed in a later chapter).

In 1908, a local newspaper reported on the dedication of the Bucktail Monument that is still standing in this little village.

> *Last Monday was a Red-Letter Day for Driftwood, the occasion being the dedication of the Bucktail Monument erected by the State of Pennsylvania at a cost of $2,500. The town was literally packed with people from all sections of the country. The "Boys" of 1861 came from all points, one from Texas and one from St. Louis. The number in attendance was fully 1,800, possibly more. The dedication exercises took place upon a large platform erected near the monument, opposite The Curtin Hotel. The shaft is of substantial granite rock, surmounted by a Bucktail Soldier with his rifle in hand....Driftwood has reason to be proud of the success of the occasion, as are also those who celebrate the crowning event of the Bucktails, because that will possibly be the last great rally until the camp-fire in the great beyond.[155]*

Driftwood was actually the first settlement made in Cameron County, previously known as Second Fork. The first settler there was John Jordan, in 1804. About forty years of age, he was known as a great hunter, which some speculate was the reason he came to this remote section of Pennsylvania. It is said he killed ninety-six elk—quite a record.[156]

According to the Census Bureau, the population of Driftwood in 2020 was thirty-six.[157] Contrast this to its earlier history of growth: when a serious fire in 1871, caused by sparks from a locomotive, nearly devastated the growing business area, Driftwood seemed to bounce back and continued to grow. "In 1910 its population was five hundred seventeen, reaching an estimated six hundred fifty by 1916. The town had lumber yards, saw mills,

Bucktail Regiment marker, Driftwood, Pennsylvania. *John Myers.*

a cannery, an aluminum cooking utensils plant, a newspaper, schools, two churches and four stores. The town also had a water system, electricity, and cement sidewalks."[158]

Driftwood was the terminus of the Allegheny Valley Railroad. Ten train crews were stationed there. Three passenger trains ran to Red Bank, Pennsylvania, and returned daily, while on the Pennsylvania Railroad, eleven passenger trains from Buffalo and Erie to Philadelphia and New York made daily stops. On the Buffalo and Susquehanna Railroad, two trains each day stopped at Driftwood. [159]

One of the most popular stores was the Brookbank Store. Next to the counter, stools were positioned five feet apart, giving clients the opportunity to sit down and rest, talk politics or just plain gossip. Outside the store, hitching posts were set up to tie up horses or oxen. The store had a big icehouse that held about one hundred sled loads of ice, each sled load weighing about one ton. This ice was used in the hand-built refrigerator in the store. Ice came from the local streams when it was about ten inches thick. Working with contracts from the Brookbank store and other businesses, it could take twenty men two weeks to cut enough ice to fill all the refrigerators in town. It took about ten teams of horses to haul the ice.[160]

One old-timer remembers merchandise in the stores, all of it ordered in bulk, in barrels and wooden boxes: pork in two-hundred-pound barrels; sugar, light or dark brown, two hundred pounds; granulated sugar, one hundred pounds, in cloth sacks; crackers, one thousand pounds, all in wooden barrels; beans, one hundred pounds, in cloth sacks; plug tobacco, in wooden boxes, fifty pounds; raisins, twenty-five pounds. A fifty-pound sack of Big A wheat flour sold for ninety cents, a fifty-pound sack of Big G sold for eighty cents and a fifty-pound sack of buckwheat flour cost seventy cents.[161]

A news article in 1960 asked,

> *Do people remember when the Pennsylvania Railroad was completed between Ridgway and Driftwood in 1862? When six passenger trains arrived from and departed to Pittsburgh daily at Driftwood? When in 1913 a tall tree was cut near Huntley and shipped to Erie to be used as a part for Perry's flagship when it was being rebuilt? When Goosetown, in the west end of Driftwood, was a settlement of Irish families who raised geese?*[162]

Bucktail State Park Natural Area. *Pennsylvania Department of Conservation and Natural Resources.*

The bustling town of yesteryear is gone. Today, with the steep hills that surround the area, visitors enjoy the Bucktail Overlook, also known as Top of the World and Mason Hill Overlook, which provides a 360-degree panoramic view of the Sinnemahoning watershed. It is also known for its "dark skies" for stargazing. The Fred Woods Trail is a scenic three-mile loop on the top of the hill.[163]

SINNEMAHONING

As mentioned in an earlier chapter, the name Sinnemahoning is a corruption of Achsinni-mahoni, "stony lick," a Native American term for the main tributary of the West Branch of the Susquehanna River.[164] For many years, the village was known as First Fork.

In 1778, during the American Revolution, an event took place in Pennsylvania known as the Great Runaway, which occurred shortly after the Wyoming Valley Massacre on July 2–3 at a fort near the Susquehanna River, in which the British and their Indian allies killed a number of soldiers and civilians. Concerned for their safety, settlers fled the Wyoming Valley region and the West Branch of the Susquehanna River to safer locations in eastern Pennsylvania.[165]

Other raids occurred throughout the region. On August 8, a man named James Brady, a relative of one Peter Grove, was killed in an Indian attack on a group of soldiers on the Loyal Sock in Lycoming County. Following this incident, Peter Grove and his brother Michael were determined to take revenge on the Indians. Accompanied by a friend, the three men located the Indians' trail and followed them to the mouth of the Tangascootak Creek (Scootack Creek), a tributary of the Susquehanna River in Clinton County, and then up the valley to the mouth of Sinnemahoning Creek.[166]

The men found the Indians camped near the mouth of what has since been named Grove's Run near the town of Sinnemahoning. Peter Grove and his companions killed eight Indians in revenge. Taking the Indians' guns, the men broke the locks and threw them into the creek before making their way back to safety in a settlers' fort. According to Beers's *History of the Counties of McKean, Elk, Cameron and Potter*, in about the year 1820, the pond at the mouth of Grove Creek where the battle occurred was drained and a gun barrel and lock were found, apparently remains from the battle between the Grove party and the Indians.[167]

George B. Stevenson Dam, Sinnemahoning State Park. *Nicholas A. Tonelli, Wikimedia Commons.*

From this somewhat violent beginning, Sinnemahoning eventually became a boomtown—logging, two railroads running through and a dynamite plant being among its early industries. Dynamite manufactured at Sinnemahoning was used in building the Panama Canal, and gunpowder manufactured there was used in World Wars I and II. Flagstone mined in the area was used to build the front of the Tomb of the Unknown Soldier at Arlington Cemetery.[168]

Life was not all work in those earlier years. During the big lumbering days through to World War I, the Independent Order of Odd Fellows (IOOF) was found in Cameron and Elk Counties, including Driftwood, Sinnemahoning and Benezette. Its commands were to "visit the sick, relieve the distressed, bury the dead and educate the orphan."[169] In other nearby locations, the Moose had a lodge, and other organizations that are almost forgotten today had active membership: the Modern Woodsmen and the Red Men, to name a couple.[170]

The men of Sinnemahoning apparently had a great sense of humor. They organized a social club known as the Sinnemahoning Liars Club, which met on a regular basis. The club was such a popular concept that other clubs were organized in the area, with competitions between them: the taller the tale, the better.

George B. Stevenson Reservoir in the Sinnemahoning State Park. *Yinan Chen, Wikimedia Commons.*

At one such meeting in 1899, George Shaffer took to the floor and said,

> *One of his cows would shake an apple tree and leave the apples until the other two cows came along when the fruit would be equally divided. If only one apple was left it would be divided into three parts. George occupied the major portion of the meeting and, as the Shaffers never have much to say ordinarily, it was a great surprise to the club. He closed his trap box with the remark that he had an imported calf from Benezette that would pull up potatoes by the top and eat the small ones and bring the large ones to the house for cooking...Harvey Smith reported that he hauled 9,600 feet of bark at one load. He was ordered to sit down, under threat of expulsion....W.H. Michaels proposed that we all accompany him to the cellar to wait for champagne. The club adjourned in disorder, all trying to get their [sic] first. In the scuffle someone stepped on O.S. Bailey's corns. He struck Pap Blodget and a general row ensued. Tom Snyder came out best, with no bones broken.*[171]

Today, the Sinnemahoning area offers 1,910 acres of beautiful scenery and outstanding opportunities for viewing wildlife at nearby Sinnemahoning

State Park, including bald eagles, coyotes, elk and bobcats.[172] The George B. Stevenson Reservoir offers 145 acres for kayaking, canoeing, boating (electric motors only) and fishing for trout, bass and panfish. There is an ADA-accessible fishing pier.[173]

Chapter 4

RELIGIOUS LEGACY

NATIVE AMERICAN BELIEFS

"When William Penn first came to America in 1682, the Delawares [Lenni Lenape] occupied the soil of southeastern Pennsylvania, but their political overlords were the Five Nations, the Iroquois Confederacy, whose homeland was in upstate New York."[174] That confederacy also included the tribe most familiar today to the inhabitants of the Pennsylvania Wilds region, the Seneca.

The Delaware eventually left southeastern Pennsylvania and settled in the Ohio Valley, which included Western Pennsylvania, but were driven out following the French and Indian War. Cornplanter, the chief of the Seneca, fought on the side of the British during the Revolution, but after the war, he urged reconciliation with the Americans.[175] Pennsylvania awarded him three tracts of land for his efforts in bringing people together, two of which he sold; the third was six hundred acres of land, most of it on the west bank of the Allegheny River just south of New York State in Warren County, Pennsylvania. In 1960, that land became part of Kinzua Dam, built primarily for flood control.

Conrad Weiser, a German settler, served as an interpreter and diplomat between the Pennsylvania Colony and the Native American Nations.[176] Regarding the beliefs of Native Americans, he said,

> *If the word religion means a formal belief in certain written Articles of Faith…then we can truly say: the Indians…have no religion.…But if by*

the word religion we understand the knitting of the soul to God, and the intimate relation to, and hunger after the highest Being arising therefrom, then we must certainly allow this apparently barbarous people a religion.[177]

In other words, Native American religion held that "all things had souls, not only man, but also animals, the air, water, trees, even rocks and stones."[178]

The Delaware believed in the Great Spirit and his agents and an afterlife. The creation of the earth was told through the story of the world on the turtle's back.[179]

Cornplanter's half-brother, Handsome Lake, brought a "New Religion" to the Seneca nation and other nations in the Iroquois Confederacy. Suffering from a moral and mental collapse following the Revolution and the breakup of the Senecas' national home, Handsome Lake became a drunk, wasting away for years hoping to die. Eventually, through what he described as a series of visions, Handsome Lake believed he received a message from the Creator about how to revitalize the Iroquois people. Preaching a message of strict morality, he told of four great sky trails leading to the "Land of Happy Spirits."[180] A prayer, offered up by Brooks Redeye, a Seneca Keeper of the Faith, in 1843, sheds light on some of the New Religion's beliefs. Redeye prayed directly to God, thanking Him for the Four Angels who guide his people day and night; he thanked the Thunders, servants of God, who nourish the earth; the Sun that God put in the sky to give light; the Moon that God put there; the Waters that God meant to keep them from thirst; the Earth that God gave them to walk on; the Trees that God placed on the land; the Grasses and Herbs for medicine.[181]

The Native American beliefs were so woven into nature that Tecumseh, a Shawnee chief and warrior, expressed their views of land ownership, which differed greatly from European views, in this way: "What. Sell land! As well sell air and water. The Great Spirit gave them in common to all."[182]

Early Settlers' Beliefs

The spiritual needs of the people were not met by formal church services or ministers in the early years of settlement in this isolated region of Pennsylvania. Some settlers held services in their homes without the benefit of clergy, bringing together people who may have come from different denominations but who shared the Christian faith. One such settler was

Peter Pearsall, who had a vision to establish a church on his property in Jay Township near Caledonia. His dream became a reality in 1856, when his son completed building the first Protestant church in Elk County, known as Mt. Zion, which is covered in another chapter in this book.

There is also another early record in Jay Township of the county's first religious service being held in 1817 by a Revolutionary War veteran, the Reverend Jonathan Nichols.[183] An ordained Baptist minister and an educated physician, Nichols settled briefly above Weedville in 1817. It was not uncommon for people to travel miles to meetings, even in winter, in sleds drawn by oxen. In summer, men, women and children would walk sometimes as far as nine or ten miles and then back home, just to hear the gospel. Known as a generous and kind-hearted man, Nichols was always ready to assist the needy. "Winter's snow never deterred him from his pastoral work or visits to the sick."[184]

In 1833, the Pine Street Presbyterian Church of Philadelphia purchased goods to supply a mission church in Cameron County. In an interview, one of the oldest settlers on the West Branch of the Susquehanna, James Caldwell, discussed his recollections about one of the first ministers of the Presbyterian faith. Daniel Barber, who was in the area in 1829, was described by Caldwell as a "gentleman of fine ability and a great religious worker."[185] The first church was established at Youngwomanstown, and settlers from ten miles around assembled there. A Sabbath school was organized and flourished for a number of years. Barber also organized churches at First Fork and Sterling Run.

Barber was followed by a Mr. Allen, who came from Jersey Shore. While he wasn't an ordained minister, there had been an absence of a minister at First Fork for some time, and Allen volunteered to preach, setting a date on a Sunday several weeks away so people would have notice to attend the services. Caldwell's story relates that people from miles around came to hear Allen out of curiosity.

Shortly after the preaching was commenced, John Jordan's boys started up a deer with their dogs, that bounded past the meeting house, within sight of the people and ran up the creek. The people all left their places and their pastor to witness the chase, which was of an exciting nature. The preacher was much perplexed at the conduct of his hearers and exclaimed, solemnly, "All in vain!" "All in vain!" meaning of course, that his flock cared more for the sport of killing a deer than they did for listening to the words of the Bible; but one of the settlers, who had grown excited over the chase failed to

*comprehend the meaning of his pastor's words, and in the way of a reply
quickly retorted, "Well, I does not know, but I thinks they'll catch him yet."
It is needless to add, continued Mr. Caldwell, that everybody saw the joke
in the German settler's reply and roared with laughter. Mr. Jordan felt very
sad over the fact that his boys did violate his injunction not to hunt on that
day,* [and would] *thrash their backs effectually when he got them home.
The boys, however, got the deer and escaped their threatened punishment.*[186]

Eventually, the Methodists moved into the area and established many
more churches than the Presbyterians. Circuit-riding Methodists made their
rounds over bad roads and through snow. A circuit rider could be based
miles away. An example of a route for one rider based in Coudersport in
1823 follows:

*Coudersport to Port Allegany, 18 miles; thence on 10 miles to dividing
ridge; then 14 miles to Portage; then down to Sinnemahoning, 24 miles;
thence 3 miles to North Creek; then 2 miles to West Creek; thence 7 miles
to Big Run; then 23 miles to Kersey; then 12 miles to Brockway; then 23
miles to Bennetts Branch and the Driftwood Branch; then 16 miles to the
mouth of the Sinnemahoning; then 15 miles to Youngwomanstown (North
Point), returning via Potato Creek and Smethport to Coudersport, a distance
of 249 miles.*[187]

Thomas Hollen was a circuit-riding minister who served in Elk and
Cameron Counties. He kept a "journal of his visits to preach in homes,
schools, churches and at revivals. He visited the sick and performed marriages
and funerals for his congregations. His life was difficult requiring traveling
long distances weekly and being called out in all kinds of weather."[188] Several
journal entries are reproduced here to give insight into his life while he was
living in Sterling Run, Cameron County.

February 15, 1860, Wednesday—was cauled [sic] *to go to Bennetts
Branch to preach a funeral went over and stayed with Bro. Barr overnight
it was a very snowy day but the Lord sustained and gave his aid.*

*February 16, 1860—Thursday—Preached James Barr funeral from
Luke 13*[th] *2 & 3 it was a solemn time and mutch* [sic] *weeping the friends
was very mutch affected Oh how hard to preach where there is no hope.*[189]

BENEZETT METHODIST CHURCH-BUILT 1870
The above picture was taken in 1965
after remodeling was completed

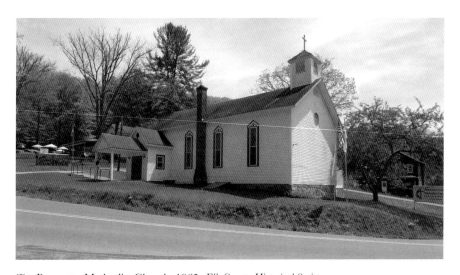

Top: Benezette Methodist Church, 1965. *Elk County Historical Society.*

Bottom: Benezette Methodist Church, 2023. *John Myers.*

August 20 1860—Monday—At Andrew Overturfs. Started for home dined at Levi Hicks met Bro Boyer there came over the hill in company with him found my family all well praise the name of the Lord.[190]

In 1871, I.S. Crone was serving the Methodist circuit in Cameron County; he observed that at Driftwood, services were held in a hired hall while a new schoolhouse was being built, and he was looking forward to the erection of a Union Protestant Church. Crone noted that an outbreak of scarlet fever took the lives of many children. But on a positive note, he said, "Our labors this year have been abundant, sometimes almost beyond our strength, but we have seen a rich harvest of souls gathered into the fold of Christ and many of God's people encouraged and revived."[191]

In the late 1800s, camp meetings and revival meetings became popular. In Sinnemahoning, there were special grounds where the camp meetings were held. Several preachers would be there, and they drew large crowds, with many traveling in by train.[192]

The *Elk County Advocate* reported on a Sunday school picnic in Weedville:

Penfield, PA, Aug. 7 1876, Editor Advocate:—About five hundred persons attended the Sunday School Institute and picnic in the pine grove of Mrs. Weed, Weedville, on the 5th inst. The occasion was one of much interest, and the whole movement did credit to the people of the valley. Excursion rates had been kindly granted by the railroad, and fully two hundred came on the trains. Thirteen teams were in our procession from above Weedville. The schools brought neat and appropriate banners. Provisions were abundant; weather splendid; the singing, praying and talking were vigorous, and all passed off in harmony and good feeling. L. Bird.[193]

Catholicism arrived in the region in 1842, when the German Union Bond Society purchased thirty-five thousand acres of land from the U.S. Land Company, and by the fall of that year, thirty-one families from Germany had settled in a new community, Marienstadt, or St. Marys, as it is known today.[194] Occasionally, a Redemptorist Father would travel throughout the region serving what few members he could find.[195] As industry developed, there was an influx of immigrants into the Benezette region, many of them Irish and Italian, who worshipped as Catholics, creating the need for regular services for those families.

One notable priest was the Right Reverend Monsignor T.F. Brennan, DD. Born near Cashel, Ireland, about 1857, he came to the United States at the

Above: St. James Catholic Church, Driftwood. *John Myers.*

Opposite, top: St. Cecelia's Catholic Church, Benezette, 1965. *Elk County Historical Society.*

Opposite, bottom: Elk Life, 2023, formerly St. Cecelia's Catholic Church. *John Myers.*

age of eight. Entering college to study for the priesthood, he spent some time at St. Bonaventure's near Olean, New York. In 1873, Brennan traveled to France to finish his classical education. From there, he went on to Germany and eventually entered the University of Innsbruck, in the Tyrol region of Austria, graduating with the title doctor of divinity. He also studied canon law in Rome. On his return, Brennan was assigned as assistant priest in Greenville, Mercer County, Pennsylvania, and later in the same capacity in DuBois, Frenchville and Driftwood, Pennsylvania.

Brennan visited Europe twice and also traveled through portions of Africa and Asia. He was a delegate to the Pope's Jubilee and eventually met the pope, who gave him the title monsignor. Brennan spoke and wrote twenty languages—an amazing scholar who, in addition to Driftwood, had charge of the Catholic church in Benezette and parishes in Sterling Run, Cameron County and Germania and Galeton, in Potter County.[196]

ST CECELIA CHURCH IN BENEZETT.
Said to be the oldest Catholic
Church in Bennett's Valley.
This church was dedicated in 1879.
Above photo as seen in 1965.

St. Cecelia's Catholic Church in Benezette was the oldest Catholic church in Bennett's Valley. Built with mostly donated labor, it was dedicated on November 23, 1879. Its first priest was the abovementioned Reverend Dr. Brennan of Driftwood. Prior to the establishment of train travel, services were held by the priest once a month. Lay ministers would lead church members on other days during the month. Eventually the church came under the Force parish, and in 1965, the church was temporarily closed, while members met once a month for evening prayers or an occasional service.

The influx of immigrants created the need for churches of different denominations and clergy to serve them. An amusing story is told involving a group of woodsmen who knew little about religion. Finding themselves "hung up" on a pier in the river and fearful they would all drown, one of the crew, a Frenchman, knelt down to pray in his native language. Observing his mate, another crew member stated, "Look at that damn fool, just as if Jesus Christ understands French."[197]

Today, many of the Methodist churches have closed, their congregations having been absorbed into other groups. St. Cecelia's Church in Benezette was sold, and today its sturdy building has been turned into Elk Life Store, offering ice cream; donuts; breakfast, lunch and dinner to go; and Elk Life apparel and merchandise.

Chapter 5

SCHOOLS

School days, school days,
Dear old golden rule days,
Readin' and 'ritin' and 'rithmetic
Taught to the tune of the hickory stick…
Let's take a trip on memory's ship
Back to the bygone days
Sail to the old village school house
Anchor outside the school door
Look in and see
There's you and there's me
A couple of kids once more.[198]

In October 2022, the St. Marys Area School District Board of Directors voted to close the Bennetts Valley Elementary School, located in Weedville. It was the culmination of a history of schooling in the Benezette region that reached back two hundred years to 1821, when the first school in Medix Run was opened, with Cephas Morey teaching three children in the village.[199]

An article published in a local newspaper in January 1881 provided a look into school life in those early days. It noted that the school at Dents Run was being taught by a veteran teacher, Lawrence Fee. It was a small school with only fourteen enrolled, and the pupils were faithful attendees.[200]

Picture Of Benezette School, 1897

The above picture of the Benezette School. during the 1897 term. | among them are: Dr. Harry Winslow, Alvan Rummer, Mike Galla-
Many of the students shown in this picture we have been unable | gher, Margaret Gallagher, Etta and Hattie Tuttle, Gertrude Greiner,

Benezette School, 1897. *Bennetts Valley News.*

The Johnson school, at Grant, was under the direction of Miss Mary Reece, with twenty-five students. The average daily attendance was twenty-one. Both the Medix Run school and the Grant school were furnished with Guyot's outline maps (elementary geography for primary classes), a map of Pennsylvania and a large blackboard. The schools were decorated with pictures and mottos.[201]

The Mt. Pleasant school, located on Winslow Hill and mentioned in an earlier chapter, was under the guidance of Miss Jennie Hyman, with about twenty-five pupils enrolled. At the time of the news article, attendance had been down due to sickness that kept children out of school, but it was improving.[202]

The Benezette graded school, as it was known, was taught by Mrs. and Mr. Frank Lenig, with Mrs. Lenig having charge of the primary grades and Mr. Lenig in charge of the high school grades. Thirty-nine were enrolled in the lower grades and forty-five in the high school. The school was outfitted with an organ in the principal's office, and both the primary school and the high school were supplied with maps, chairs and blackboards.[203]

Dents Run school was taught by Miss Lenora Whiting, with twenty-one enrolled. The schoolhouse was a model, with the *Elk County Advocate* noting that Miss Whiting was the right person in the right place.[204]

The newspaper article quoted George R. Dixon, county superintendent of schools at the time. He offered suggestions as well:

> *To Teachers—Teach more by way of general lessons. Secure, if possible, a better attendance. Give more thorough attention to writing. Preserve the manuscript work of the pupils and exhibit it to visitors. To Directors— Keep the text books uniform. Put patent furniture into the school houses as fast as the old desks wear out. To parents—Send the children to school more regularly.* [205]

By June 1881, the newspaper was cheering on the Benezette school district. An article reported that of the six schoolrooms in the district, only one of them was furnished with patent furniture (manufactured school desks that were made under design patents). The directors determined to furnish all the schoolrooms with the latest and most approved desks and seats, including first-class teachers' desks and recitation benches. Each school would receive a copy of the latest edition of *Webster's Unabridged Dictionary*. The article concluded by asking: What other school board would do the same? [206]

One humorous account of readin', 'ritin' and 'rithmetic is found in *Sinnemahone: A Story of Great Trees and Powerful Men* by George William Huntley:

> *A young couple from Reesville came to Sinnemahoning to get married. The minister was a young man who had recently come to the circuit. He took the ceremony very seriously and undertook to carry out all the prescribed requirements. The young couple stood up before him and he asked the young man if he were a citizen of the United States. He replied, "No, sir, I am from Potter County." He asked the young woman the same question and she replied, "No, sir, I am from Potter County." "Then I cannot marry you because I have no authority to marry foreigners," said the preacher. Emma Hall taught school at Reesville that winter. She was a tactful and dignified young lady with a fine education. Whenever the natives had a problem they could not solve, they sent it to the school teacher. She was looked upon as the Book of Knowledge for the whole community. They referred to her questions in mathematics, science, literature, and government. However, they did not refer questions on religion and astronomy, because the Reesville gentry yielded to nobody on any question that could be proved by the Holy Bible and Jayne's Almanac. She patiently answered all questions and by that means held their confidence. Returning home the young couple called on the wise schoolmarm to solve their problem. She explained to them that*

BENEZETT SCHOOL that was erected
in 1905. The above picture was
taken after the announcement was
made that the school would be
permanently closed in 1965

Benezette School after its closing was announced in 1965. *Elk County Historical Society.*

*they were citizens of the United States, even if they were born and reared in
Potter County, and that they should go back to the preacher and show him
that the people who came from Potter County were not foreigners. They went
back and took the schoolmarm for a witness; then they were married. The
preacher "fell" for the teacher, and here the story ends.*[207]

In Benezette, the old frame building that was the original school was
destroyed by fire in 1904. The following year, a modern brick structure was
erected and served the community until 1965. In the 1930s and '40s, as the
small schools began to close, the school in Benezette became the center of
learning for the township.[208]

To provide a better curriculum and teaching facilities, a jointure was formed with nearby Jay Township in 1952, and two years later, the senior high school was moved to Weedville. In 1958, with the completion of a new junior-senior high school building in Weedville, the Benezette Junior High School was also moved to that town.[209]

This jointure did not last long. In 1965, at the commonwealth's direction and due to local financial considerations, a merger was made with the St. Marys Area School District. The school district came under the supervision of a nine-area board of directors with one tax structure. All junior-senior high school students were then transported to St. Marys.[210] The most recent action by the St. Marys Area School District in 2022, to close the elementary school, brought an end to teaching in the Benezette region. The school district has agreed to turn the Weedville school over to Jay Township.

A group of civic-minded residents in the Benezette region has formed a Benezette School Committee to provide support for the old Benezette schoolhouse. Each October, it hosts an Elktoberfest that welcomes many vendors to the region. Proceeds from this event are used for maintenance of

Benezette School, 2023. *John Myers.*

the building, and in July 2023, the committee provided Benezette Township with a $10,000 donation to replace the building's thirty-year-old roof.[211] The building is currently used as a municipal building and for elections. The cornerstone of the 1881 building can be found in the basement of the 1905 Benezette School.

In Weedville, after the closure of the Bennetts Valley Elementary School mentioned at the beginning of this section, which ended two hundred years of teaching in the Benezette region, the St. Marys Area School District, in June 2023, gifted the building to Jay Township.

Elktoberfest medallion. *Kathy Myers.*

Members of the community are credited for their involvement in making this happen. John Bricen, a local resident, said, "It's been a long, hard, sometimes contentious, back-and-forth between the citizens of BV [Bennett's Valley] and the board. This school means a lot. I graduated from there; my kids graduated from there. We're going to take it and make it something good again." Future "plans are to use it for township offices, but mostly as a community center and ensure that it 'remains the cornerstone' of their beloved community."[212]

Population shifts as well as jointures in school districts also affected other villages in the Benezette Corridor. Hicks Run School closed in 1930, Mix Run in 1938, Castle Carden School in 1959 and Driftwood Elementary School in 1966. Students eventually were consolidated in the Emporium Public Schools.

Chapter 6

INDUSTRY

Lumber

*The clank of metal, the shouts of men, and the thunderous collapse of trees
are merely echoes in the forests....Around the turn of the twentieth century,
the lumbering business was big...Across the heavily forested region of
north central Pennsylvania. Eager entrepreneurs, followed by a caravan of
tavern owners, teachers, pastors, and craftsmen, moved into the woodlands
to log the white pine and hemlock trees. Across the state, busy lumber towns
were quickly established and, once the supply of timber had been exhausted,
were just as quickly abandoned.*[213]

At its founding, Pennsylvania was heavily forested—90 percent of the state,
according to one estimate. The state, including this region, was covered by
a combination of white pine, eastern hemlock and assorted hardwoods.[214]

Even today, this region is known for its lumber industry, and it is not unusual
to pass trucks carrying logs to market as you make your way down the Elk
Scenic Drive, Route 555. In nearby McKean County, Kane, Pennsylvania,
is known as the black cherry capital of the world.[215]

In the earliest of times, timber was harvested to build cabins and barns.
Some enterprising settlers took part in timbering as a secondary occupation:
for example, Levi Hicks, who floated the first raft down the Sinnemahoning
Creek.[216] Men like Hicks became known as farmer-raftsmen. The woods
provided work during the slack season. Logs were cut and skidded into the

Rafting on the Susquehanna. *Library of Congress.*

stream over winter snows and then floated to market as rafts during the spring floods. Generally, the rafts were made of square-cut timber. The rafts also provided a way of transporting farm products to market, which resulted in the clearing of more farmland to earn money to buy products made in the settled regions where the logs were sold.[217]

The mid-nineteenth century saw major changes take place in the methods used by the lumber industry that dated to the founding of the nation. Early settlers along the coast had used the rich forests of North America for building materials, firewood, charcoal and wood potash. "By 1775, however plentiful it may be in the remoter parts of Pennsylvania…wood is almost as dear at Philadelphia as it is in some parts of Britain."[218]

To find more timber in Pennsylvania, by 1830, logging was well established on the West Branch of the Susquehanna River, including its tributaries, the Sinnemahoning Creek and the Bennett's Branch.[219]

Rafting grew into a major business, with the average raft being 150 to 300 feet long by 24 feet wide. Each raft was manned by a first and second steersman and a first and second pilot. The oars, generally made from hemlock timber, were about 20 feet long, and each oar was fastened to a

Lɒɢ Rᴀꜰᴛs ɪɴ ᴛʜᴇ Sᴜsqᴜᴇʜᴀɴɴᴀ Rɪᴠᴇʀ ᴀᴛ Lᴏᴄᴋ Hᴀᴠᴇɴ, Pᴀ.

Lock Haven log rafts.
Wikimedia Commons.

spiked, tapering plank from 14 to 16 feet long in order to balance it. Loaded, the average raft carried 5,000 feet of timber.[220]

The Sinnemahoning region became well-known for one particular branch of logging, the spar business. For you landlubbers unfamiliar with the term, spars were used in building sailing vessels. While spars was a small part of the logging business in the region, its specialty was based on the giant trees that were found there.[221] One spar measured in a spar contest by a timber surveyor was "one hundred and twenty feet long, twenty-three inches in diameter at the top end, and contained six thousand feet board measure. He [the timber surveyor] predicted it would be the largest stick of timber ever taken out on the Sinnemahoning waters."[222]

Sawmills sprang up in many of the villages in the Benezette region along the Route 555 corridor. In the spring of 1816, the first sawmill on the Bennett's Branch was built at the mouth of Kersey Run in Weedville.[223]

Logging was hard work, and it was not unusual for the men involved in the business to spend long days in the woods, cutting the trees, skidding them down the sides of mountains, peeling the bark by hand and cutting square timber, among other tasks. The lumbermen were known as "wood hicks" and followed strict rules in the camps, many of which enforced a strict nine o'clock lights out time and zero tolerance for alcohol. In some camps, workers were forbidden to speak to each other during mealtimes.[224] Sanitary conditions in the lumbering camps were less than desirable. Many times, the sleeping quarters were crowded and had very little ventilation. The springs from which water was carried in jugs were unprotected, and all the men drank from the same drinking cup. There were no privies and no means of bathing. The men went long periods without a bath or a change of clothes.[225]

Emporium Lumber at Benzinger. *Pennsylvania Lumber Museum, Pennsylvania Historic and Museum Commission.*

Lumber camp boardinghouse. *Courtesy of Library of Congress.*

Room and board, so to speak, were part of the workmen's wages, and the logging operator who could furnish the best food could draw and hold the best crew. The laborers who traveled from camp to camp kept informed about the food in the different camps. Word of the best "grub" was passed along in barroom discussions during the wood hicks' "social time."[226] The wood hicks didn't care about the appearance of a male cook or his cookroom but would not tolerate a female cook who was untidy in her physical appearance or in the cookroom. They were, however, courteous to the female cooks. Which cooks were hired depended on the size of the crew. A timber-rafting business with a smaller crew would hire a woman cook, while the crews that were sawing logs may have had fifty to one hundred men, and food preparation for that number of men required larger kettles, skillets and pans to be handled—an easier chore for men.[227]

The cooks did the ordinary cooking but also all the baking of bread, cakes and pies. The cook was assisted by a helper in the cookroom who was called the "cookee." The cookee washed dishes, waited on tables, peeled potatoes, washed towels, packed lunches and called the men to meals. It was his responsibility to call the men out of bed in time for breakfast, which was served while it was still dark. It was important for every camp foreman to have his job run smoothly, with the men getting an early breakfast so there was no delay in getting them to work on time.[228] In some camps, an additional helper was used to care for the bunkhouse. Known as the lobby hog, that person made up bunks, swept the floors, cleaned the lamps and kept the camp supplied with water and wood. In camps where there was no lobby hog, the cookee was assigned these additional responsibilities.[229]

Traveling through the Benezette region today, it is almost incomprehensible to grasp the extent of the logging business in those earlier times.

Recalling the rafting days on the West Branch of the Susquehanna, one old-timer said there were so many rafts that one "was touching oars with other rafts every five minutes."[230] It has been estimated that thirty thousand men rafted on the West Branch of the Susquehanna each year, with individual raftsmen making several trips in a season. In 1857, it was reported that five hundred rafts were tied up at Lock Haven at one time. Counting the crew on the rafts, the men working in the woods to fell the timber and those involved in getting the timber into the river and downstream, the number of those involved may have actually exceeded thirty thousand.

From the early years of rafting, times began to change—slowly at first. In 1836, a man known as John Leighton came from Maine to investigate the West Branch of the Susquehanna and its potential for lumbering. Having

Above: Cameron County Star Box Company Lumber Yard near Sinnemahoning. *Courtesy of the Pennsylvania State Archives.*

Left: Pennsylvania lumberjacks at work. *Courtesy of Library of Congress.*

Opposite: John DuBois Jr. *Courtesy of* History of Clearfield County, Pennsylvania, *by Lewis Cass Aldrich.*

experience with a "boom" in Penobscot, Maine, he recognized that water above Williamsport was ideal for a massive log boom.[231] A log boom is a barrier placed in a river to collect or contain floating logs. Lacking financial backers, in 1844, he persuaded James H. Perkins of Lincoln, Maine, to visit Williamsport. Perkins became the main force in constructing a boom there. One other well-known figure in the history of this region of Pennsylvania joined them in their efforts: John DuBois Jr., founder of the city of DuBois, located approximately thirty miles from Benezette.

John DuBois Jr. was born near Owego in Tioga County, New York, on March 3, 1809, the second in a family of thirteen children. His father, John DuBois, claimed he was a descendant of the Huguenots of France. His father has been described as a man of decision, tall, with a commanding presence. His mother, Lucy, was a descendant of early settlers of the Susquehanna Valley. Lucy ruled her family with a firm hand, encouraging her children through her example and guidance.[232]

DuBois and some of his brothers entered into the lumber business near their home region, where they gained experience in the lumbering methods of the early pioneers. As the supply of pine timber diminished, DuBois began to look for a new area of operation, and he and his brothers, David and Matthias, purchased land and a mill site on Lycoming Creek, in Pennsylvania. As quickly as their capital increased, they purchased five hundred acres on the south side of the river opposite the upper end of Williamsport. In a few years, this became the location of large steam gang mills and extensive lumberyards.[233]

Following the death of their brother David, Matthias and John purchased land in Clearfield County that had some of the finest pine timber in Pennsylvania. These lands were inaccessible for immediate lumbering operations, but the brothers assumed the burden of no return and the risk of fires over a period of years for what they expected they would eventually gain from their investment. At the death of Matthias, who was his partner, John DuBois purchased his brother's interests in the business, lands and other property, leaving him the sole owner and manager of what had grown into a large business.[234]

Log boom on the
Susquehanna River.
*Courtesy of the Pennsylvania
State Archives.*

John DuBois, James H. Perkins and John Leighton joined together with other lumbermen in Williamsport and organized in an effort to make Williamsport the great lumber center of Pennsylvania. They secured a charter for a boom on the Susquehanna River to catch and hold logs that would be floated from the headwaters of the stream.[235] "Completed in 1851, the Williamsport Log Boom, which held hundreds of thousands of logs until they were needed by local sawmills, enabled Williamsport to become the 'Lumber Capital of the World' in the late 1800s. At its peak, the boom's six miles of walls could hold close to a million logs in a 450-acre enclosure. The boom remained in place until 1909, when its dismantling ended the water era of sawmilling in Williamsport."[236]

This shift from rafting-style logging to floating the logs downriver to be captured in the boom caused severe clashes between the traditional raftsmen and the modernization of the timber industry. In 1850, one year before the completion of a permanent boom, a temporary boom was in place. Four years before, a violent storm had blown down a large stand of timber along Moshannon Creek, a tributary of the West Branch. The timber was too broken to furnish the long logs needed for rafting, so its owner, Portland Lumber Company of Maine, hired an experienced log driver to cut the timber into short, sixteen-foot logs that were best for driving and float them out in the spring floods. In the spring, J.B. Wing and his crew drove more than two million feet of logs down the Moshannon to the West Branch of the Susquehanna and into the temporary boom at Williamsport.[237]

It was the beginning of the end of old-time rafting. And the industry didn't die a quiet death. There was friction between the raftsmen and the log drivers; some raftsmen turned to sabotage to discourage further drives. One of the most common forms of sabotage was "ironing" logs, which meant driving old spikes, horseshoes or other scrap metal into logs until they were hidden by the bark. The effect of this effort was realized when

Skidway of more than three thousand logs above railroad tracks, somewhere in Pennsylvania, circa 1900. *Pennsylvania State Archives.*

high-speed saws struck the iron object in the sawmill. The drivers found a way to subvert this practice: peeling logs, which revealed hidden metal. This also made for an easier way to handle the timber in the woods and mills because there was less friction on peeled logs. By 1852, legislation had been introduced to ban log drives from the Susquehanna and its tributaries. Citizens were for and against the bill, and it failed after a single no vote in the Senate.[238]

The local region was not immune to the rancor between the logging groups. In 1854, Hiram Woodward of Penfield bought Wilson & Hoyt, a company involved in lumbering. Prior to that time, someone had tried to float unpeeled logs down the Bennett's Branch but failed. Woodward believed that large numbers of logs could be floated, and he set out to show how to do it. It was an unpopular idea among some settlers. Evidence points to three men, John Lindermuth, Robert Roderick and Reuben Winslow, as having encouraged the settlers to oppose Woodward's plan. Supposedly, the three were interested in cutting timber locally and rafting it downriver. In the spring of 1855, when Woodward had a contract to drive logs down the river, the opposition to his plan was so intense that obstructions were put in the way of the drivers. Accompanying Woodward on this journey was John DuBois Jr., investor in the Williamsport boom. The two men used a raft that had a shanty built on it. When the raft reached the narrows below Caledonia, a very swift, rough and dangerous passage, the crew found a rope or a cable stretched across the stream, fastened on both sides of the shore. As the raft approached the cable, Woodward managed to step over it. DuBois attempted to cut it with his axe, but slipping, he fell. Regaining his stance just as the shanty reached the rope, DuBois struck again, severing the rope/cable, and the raft passed through in safety. On either side of the stream, an infuriated crowd opposed to Woodward and DuBois hurled objects at the crew.[239]

Left: "A Forest's Remains," somewhere in Pennsylvania, 1918. *Pennsylvania State Archives.*

Below: Regrowth of timber today. *John Myers.*

That same year, a jam occurred again in the narrows below Caledonia. In this instance, the same opposition took to spiking the timber: that is, driving spikes into all the logs they could conveniently get at. Arrests and rearrests occurred.[240]

DuBois and Woodward, again that spring, while at the mouth of Sinnemahoning Creek and about to enter the Susquehanna River, were confronted by a gang of river pirates who had come in from Reading. The ringleader struck at DuBois with a heavy pike pole. Fortunately for DuBois, it was caught by Woodward, which prevented DuBois from being knocked into the river, where the blow and the danger in the water among logs may have proven fatal. DuBois and Woodward chased the ringleader, who eluded them and made his escape.[241]

Clashes in other areas resulted in court cases with fines. Some raftsmen continued to operate not because they could compete but because they specialized in spars, delivering them to Marietta in Lancaster County or to Port Deposit, Maryland, to fill the needs of shipbuilders and others who needed large timbers. Others competed by serving the local market. Additional booms were eventually built on the river, at Lock Haven and Pine Creek, among other places.[242] Interestingly, the next challenge the Williamsport lumbermen had to face was not from the farmer-raftsmen but from workers seeking shorter hours. The first major strike in the U.S. lumber industry was at Williamsport in 1872.[243]

Railroads

The introduction of railroads into the region changed the way timber was delivered to market. In 1846, just three years after Elk County was established as a separate county, a letter was written by Leonard Morey and Henry Souther to Ignatius Garner, notifying him of his appointment as a delegate to the Philadelphia railroad convention of 1847. The convention was called to consider the completion of the Sunbury & Erie Railroad.

In 1851, a railroad meeting was held in St. Marys, and $15,500 in subscriptions was collected. Leading citizens from Ridgway and Benezette were also in favor of completion of the railroad. By 1852, a convention of delegates had been held and the various county commissioners were instructed to subscribe to the stock of the Sunbury & Erie Railroad Company, with a $100,000 subscription amount authorized, subject to confirmation by a meeting of citizens to be held in October. The meeting ratified the actions of the commissioners, with additional funds being raised to meet the subscription goals for stock in the Allegheny Valley Railroad.[244]

Thomas L. Kane, who was also the founder of the famous Civil War unit the Bucktails, was one of the directors of the Philadelphia and Erie Railroad Company and brought railroads into Elk and McKean Counties. In 1869, S. Wimmer, who had come to Elk County in 1863 as principal assistant engineer to complete a section of the Philadelphia and Erie Railroad, took charge of building the Benezette and Driftwood division of the Low Grade and, eventually, of the railway from Benezette to DuBois, which was completed in 1874.[245] Various other companies built railroads through other sections of the county, ushering in a new era of transportation in the region.

Emporium Lumber at Benzinger. *Pennsylvania Lumber Museum, Pennsylvania Historic and Museum Commission.*

Reuben Winslow, early pioneer and founder of Benezette, was invested in large amounts of timber and coal lands. He realized his competitors who were using the Philadelphia and Erie Railroad had an advantage over him, and he decided to build a railroad of his own. Securing a charter from the Pennsylvania Legislature in 1862 under the name Winslow Colliery, he gained the right to build a railroad from the Philadelphia and Erie Railroad into Elk County. In 1864, an amendment was granted permitting him to extend his railroad through Clearfield and Jefferson Counties. Winslow laid out a railroad some distance west of the summit of Sandy Lick Creek and Bennett's Branch and began construction operations for his line, as well as building a tunnel at nearby Sabula.[246]

Winslow's ambitions didn't end with the Benezette region. In 1866, his engineer, J.M. McMinn, met with influential residents of Brookville, Pennsylvania, where he laid out the benefits of a proposed railroad. The attending members of the community, after asking questions and expressing their views, agreed that bringing the railroad to Brookville would be beneficial for the community. A committee was appointed to solicit subscriptions for stock in the Winslow Colliery Company.[247] By April 1868, a Brookville newspaper had reported that arrangements for building the

Winslow Colliery Railroad and its connections had been completed, several portions of the heavy work on Bennett's Branch had been authorized and approaches to the summit tunnel at Sabula had begun.[248] But the excitement was short-lived.

Further reporting announced that the Pennsylvania Railroad Company had secured the services of Franklin Wright, who had been chief engineer of the Allegheny Valley Railroad, and a Mr. Dempster, who had also been employed by the Allegheny Valley Railroad, to work with Mr. Campbell, a contractor connected with the Pennsylvania Railroad Company, and go to the Bennett's Branch and Sabula tunnel area. Once there, they found the Winslow Colliery Company at work. In a competitive move, they adopted an alternative line that had been designed for the Allegheny Valley Railroad as their line. Without preliminary surveys on the part of the Pennsylvania Railroad Company, Wright made Campbell in charge of the line. Men were put to work, ground broken and formal possession taken of the alternative Allegheny Valley line. In the meantime, the Allegheny Valley Railroad sent its chief engineer, Mr. Martin, to the site to demand Campbell stop work on the Pennsylvania Railroad line, notifying the workers that they were trespassing. Campbell refused to leave, and the work proceeded. Martin also put his men to work, and the two rival companies maintained possession of the same ground. Expected to reach the area being worked by the Winslow Colliery Company in a few days, the Winslow men vowed that they would maintain their rights by force if necessary.[249]

Research has not revealed whether the workers actually came to blows with each other. What did happen was that the Allegheny Valley Railroad, in 1869, by special act of the state legislature, secured an amendment to its charter authorizing it to issue bonds of $10 million to build a railroad through the same territory where the Winslow Colliery Company was constructing a road. The act read as follows:

> *Whereas, it is a matter of much public importance to the state at large, that a railway should be completed at an early date, connecting the valleys of the Allegheny and the Ohio with the valleys of the East Branch of the Susquehanna, by a system of low gradients, for the movement of heavy traffic, thereby developing a valuable portion of this commonwealth and adding greatly to taxable values for state purposes, as well as to provide, in connection therewith, for the absolute security and final payment of the principal of three and a half millions of dollars, originally owing from the Sunbury and Erie Railroad Company, for the purchase of certain portions of*

the original state canals, together with interest thereon from January first, one thousand eight hundred and seventy-two. And whereas, it is believed that these desirable objects may be accomplished in order to grant sufficient authority for effective efforts, to be made to secure the same, Be it enacted, etc.[250]

The *Philadelphia Press* and the *United States Railroad and Mining Journal* gave their support to the Allegheny Valley Railroad. Locally, the boldness of agents of the Allegheny Valley Railroad in building a competitive line was questioned, with supporters of the Winslow Colliery Railroad noting that a large amount of money had been expended by the Winslow Colliery Railroad for surveys and preparations for active work and forcing them into court.[251]

It appears that the legislature originally approved the Winslow Colliery Railroad to build a line to connect its lands with the Philadelphia and Erie Railroad but required that it not interfere with the right of the Allegheny Valley Railroad to also connect with the Philadelphia and Erie Railroad.[252] Eventually, in 1869, the dispute between the Pennsylvania Railroad, Allegheny Valley and the Winslow Colliery Railroad was settled.[253]

Ironically, Reuben Winslow was killed in a train accident on the Philadelphia and Erie Railroad near Lock Haven, Pennsylvania, on April 26, 1871.

A low-grade section of the Allegheny Valley Railroad that began in 1869 later became known as the Pennsylvania Railroad, then the Conrail Line. It went from Driftwood to DuBois and beyond, with stations along the way at Grant, Summerson, Benezette, Caledonia, Weedville, Cardiff's Major Station and Penfield. The B&O line was on the other side of Bennett's Branch, providing passenger and freight services to Medix Run, and beyond the Benezette Corridor to Summerville, Brookville, Reynoldsville and fourteen minor stations.[254]

Doodlebug or hoodlebug, running from Dents Run to Wilmer. *Bennetts Valley News.*

Not to be overlooked in the history of railroading in the region was the self-propelled railcar known as the doodlebug or hoodlebug, named for its slow speed of travel. Designed to carry passengers and freight, it very often carried baggage, mail and express mail.[255]

In the Benezette region, the hoodlebug, as it was locally known, provided transportation between Dents Run and Wilmer, now a ghost town, which was once a thriving coal community.

The arrival of the railroads spurred the growth of the timber and coal industries, and they became an important part of the economic life of the region.

COAL

The Winslow coal veins were among the first mined in Benezette Township near Trout Run and Spring Run, and at the head of Autens and Dents Run. The place was known as the Winslow Colliery.[256] The word *colliery*, a British term, is little used in the United States, but according to *Merriam-Webster's Dictionary*, it means "a coal mine and its connected buildings." An 1863 examination of the coal beds showed several veins of good coal.[257]

Coal mining was a major industry in the region. In addition to the Winslow Colliery veins, mines were operated on the lands of others with familiar names: Tuttle, Cain, Winslow and Mowrey.[258] The first deep mine (or drift mine) operation in Benezette Township was opened by Gallagher in 1937.[259]

In 1947, a company from Nebraska, Hershey, Martin and Day Construction Company, began the first stripping project in the Benezette area. The company operated what is known as a walking drag, an electrically operated line with a 110-foot boom, reportedly erected at a cost of $750,000. Two years later, the P&N Coal Company from Punxsutawney, Pennsylvania, acquired strip mining rights in the area.[260]

About seven miles north of Benezette, a mining town was constructed in 1900, known as Wilmer. Ironically, the village was named for a lumbering firm, Williams and Merrill, Wilmer being a combination of the two names. At its peak, 200 miners from town and the region were employed there. The town itself had a population of 250. Serving the people in the community, Wilmer had its own country store, recreation hall and baseball team.[261]

EARLY MINING OPERATIONS

Coal mining in Pennsylvania. *Pennsylvania Department of Environmental Protection.*

In 1947, the New Shawmut Mining Company opened its first mechanical mine at Caledonia, located in Jay Township, employing thirty-two miners.[262] Other mining companies were operating nearby in other Jay Township communities, such as Cardiff, Byrnedale, Weedville and Force.[263] The Bucktail Mine was opened in Weedville in 1916 and closed in 1926. The Betta Mine, south of Weedville, which became known as the Glen Fisher Coal Company, was started in 1929 and employed approximately forty miners, reportedly doing a yearly business of $1 million.[264]

Coal was first mined with picks and shovels. Over time, methods improved, and punching machines were used, which operated by air pressure. Cutting machines were used to undercut the coal with the remaining coal drilled and blasted with dynamite. In later years, large mines used the continuous miner, which cuts the coal and moves it to a conveyor and then to the coal tipple, a structure that was used to load the coal for transportation out of the area by rail and, later, by truck. In the early days, coal was moved from the mine to the tipple by mules pulling carts.[265]

With the transition to strip mining that began in 1947, production eventually ceased in the local mines. The people in the villages actively employed in the mines looked for other jobs, many working in the nearby town of St. Marys and in the carbon industry.

The mining of coal brought on another business: the production of coke, which is a by-product of coal. In 1880, coke was manufactured at Glen Fisher, between Weedville and Caledonia, where one hundred beehive coke ovens were constructed.[266]

The Elk Coal and Coke Company, which leased about one thousand acres from the Caledonia Coal Company, operated a coking plant at Glen Fisher, producing a fine grade of coke. The company was so successful that "it has sold the entire output of 100 ovens for years to come."[267] Today, the empty beehive coke ovens remain in an overgrown area of the former operations.

Making coke was hot, backbreaking work. "The coking process consists of heating coal in the absence of air to drive off the volatile compounds; the resulting coke is a hard, but porous carbon material that is used for reducing the iron in the blast furnace."[268] The first step in the process was to fill the ovens with the mined coal. This was done using a larry car, a car that ran on a track on the top of the ovens. In the early years, these cars were powered by men or horse or mule power. Later, small steam engines were utilized and,

Beehive coke oven. *Wikimedia Commons.*

eventually, electric cars. It took one and a half tons of coal, which weighed between four and five and a half tons, to yield one ton of coke.

Once the coal was inserted in the oven, it had to be leveled, which was done by hand with a large, toothless rake attached to a long handle. Sealing the front opening was the next step, done by a mason. The mortar mix contained some of the coke dust. A typical burn time could be forty-eight to seventy-two hours, depending on the amount of coal inserted into the oven and the size of the oven's opening. Temperatures reached two thousand degrees Fahrenheit.

After the coal was changed into coke, the oven had to be carefully opened, allowing time for the coke to cool down before taking it to prepare it for market. Once cooled, it was loaded onto railroad cars by hand, for shipment to steel foundries.[269]

GAS BOOM

An obituary in a Clearfield, Pennsylvania newspaper tells an incredible story of the effects of the natural gas boom in the Benezette region on an elderly resident:

Man, Made Rich by Gas Boom, Dies

An 80-year-old mountain recluse, who became the wealthiest land-owner in the Benezette gas field, died Friday night in the Maple Avenue Hospital here, a victim of the heat wave. Quenn D. Johnson of Grant, succumbed at 9:30 p.m., about a day after he was stricken by a heat stroke while strolling around the gas rigs on his property that were reportedly bringing him $1,000 daily. And he has no survivors....When the natural gas boom swept into the Benezette field from Driftwood, [the] Johnson-owned property was among the first to be leased. All drillings on the property are productive.

He was half-owner in two wells producing on the Johnson Estate, one of such is producing 16 million cubic feet daily, and the other 10 million.

On land owned entirely by himself, a well of the Keta Gas & Oil Company is producing 10 million feet daily. Another well is reportedly producing on his land.

Until the time he began receiving royalties from the gas, Johnson had been receiving state assistance.[270]

Pennsylvania has long been known for the production of oil and natural gas, in particular northwest Pennsylvania, where in 1859, Colonel Drake drilled the first successful well near Titusville, Crawford County. That success led to prospecting for oil in other areas of Pennsylvania, and Elk County lands were included in the search. One such well was located one mile west of Benezette, on the Julius Jones farm. It was drilled in 1882, and speculators had high hopes for its production, but by 1890, the well had been cleaned out when prices dropped in the region, and it was abandoned. By the 1890s, gas was being produced in Elk County.[271] Today, gas is being produced through a new method, drilling and hydraulic fracture of the rock in the Marcellus Shale formations.

According to statistics released by the U.S. Energy Information Administration in November 2022, Pennsylvania's marketed natural gas production, primarily from the Marcellus Shale, reached a record 7.6 trillion cubic feet in 2021, making Pennsylvania the nation's second-largest natural gas producer after Texas.[272]

The year 1950 brought in a new boom to the region when a natural gas well, drilled in nearby Clinton County, caught the attention of people in the Benezette area. Known as the Leidy field, it was drilled against expert advice by Dorcie Calhoun, who hit natural gas on January 8, 1950. At a depth of 5,659 feet, for a time, it produced an estimated 15 million cubic feet of gas per day.[273]

As the Clinton County field slowed, drilling operations crept up the Susquehanna River to Driftwood and to Mix Run, both located in Cameron County. It was estimated that there were approximately one hundred drilling rigs in this early field.

The first well in Benezette Township was drilled on Woodring land in Grant in 1953. In Medix Run, drilling rigs were erected back-to-back. The hills around the township took on a new look, with roads, pipeline rights-of-way and locations set aside for drilling equipment.[274] In late 1953, another well drilled in the Medix Run vicinity brought in a gas flow of eight to ten million cubic feet per day.[275]

The impact on the region was immediate. The wells brought in a number of workers from other states: West Virginia, Texas, Oklahoma and California, among others. Hundreds of people took up residence where they could find shelter: in trailers, old abandoned houses, camps and even tents. Families coming from states with warm climates were unprepared for the winter climate and winter driving. The schools were overrun, with the student population increasing by 50 percent. Safety was another concern, and it was reported that the gas fields averaged one death per month for eight months, due to gas explosions, fires and vehicle accidents.[276] One such death reported in a local newspaper in 1954 was that of Foster Ottberry, twenty-nine, of Eldorado, Texas, who burned to death at a newly drilled gas well in Medix Run when it caught fire.[277]

The Pennsylvania Geologic Survey estimated that the Driftwood-Benezette natural gas boom would last twice as long as the Leidy field did in nearby Clinton County. The state took some credit for the longevity of the gas strike, noting that most of the 21,000 acres of land in the field was owned by the state, which had been leasing them to private firms for drilling. Noting that there was no specific spacing requirement in the contract, a commonwealth spokesman said it was understood that the wells shouldn't be drilled too close together. The commonwealth was seeing a rate of one well every 200 acres, whereas at the Leidy field twenty miles away, a single acre of land had several wells. By 1954, the Pennsylvania Department of Forest and Waters said, $4,459,000 in gas royalties had been collected in two years, which was nearly equal to the acquisition cost of its entire 1.8-million-acre forest system. In 1953, gas flowed from the Driftwood-Benezette field at the rate of 300 million cubic feet a day.[278]

While the Department of Forest and Waters was pleased with the results in Cameron and Elk Counties, in 1954, landowners from Medix Run protested its announcement of restrictions on the amount of gas permitted to flow through pipelines that crossed state property.

Medix Run landowners, believing they were on the verge of receiving a bonanza from their properties, were hemmed in on both sides by the major landowner in the area, the state government. When the state gave its right-of-way over state lands to the major gas companies in the area, stipulating that only three million cubic feet of gas could be taken from the wells, this included gas from the wells on lands owned privately. The state was receiving more than 50 percent royalties from the half-dozen wells on state lands and exporting its full capacity, while the wells on private land were held to the three million cubic feet standard.[279] The restriction affected about forty-two landowners in the Medix Run area, many of whose properties had been held by their families for generations.

The landowners hired attorney Ross Ferraro of Brockway, whose family had a camp in the Medix Run area, to be their legal representative. Ferraro was a graduate of Duquesne University and Dickinson School of Law. He became familiar with the Department of Forests and Waters while working on a flood control project in Brockway.

At a meeting of landowners held at the Logan Hotel in DuBois, Ferraro noted, "Medix Run will be the battle-ground against economic socialism." Other prominent people served on a committee to take the protest on restrictions to Harrisburg. One committee member said, "It was private capital, not the money from the Forest and Waters that developed the gas boom in Medix Run and we plan to expose this whole affair." The landowners stressed that the restrictions placed by the Department of Forests and Waters would put an end to private enterprise.[280]

The meeting in Harrisburg took place with Governor John Fine, representatives of the Department of Forests and Waters, attorney Ferraro, the committee representing Medix Run and state legislators from Clearfield, Jefferson, Cambria and other northern counties. The landowners were pleased to have the governor's ear and to know that the Department of Forests and Waters would not be able to run all over them.

By 1965–66, the boom that began in the mid-'50s had slowed, with some wells still producing but at a greatly reduced scale. Of three pump stations erected during those years, two were still in use, one at the mouth of Little Medix and the other above Sullivan Run on the road to Quehanna.[281]

Chapter 7

THE CIVIL WAR YEARS

THE BUCKTAIL REGIMENT

'Twas the month of April, in eighteen sixty-one,
That our Union's Flag was threatened by the fall of Sumter's guns;
Each loyal heart was beating true and waiting for commands.
To shoulder arms and give their lives to save their native land.
Among the hosts of patriots who heard their country's call,
Were a band of hardy mountain men, a sturdy race and tall.
Who volunteered their services, these men of daring deeds,
And only waited for a man, they, to the front to lead.
A leader came, a soldier true, all honor to his name,
This man was one of nature's best, 'twas Thomas Leiper Kane.
He was a man of sterling worth, a natural soldier born,
Who knew these mountain men from birth, and loved them as his sons.
From Elk and Cameron and McKean, these sturdy men came forth.
With Kane to guide through fire and flame as they fought for the North.
Their deeds are known by young and old, their names are household words.
These patriots who volunteered to fight with gun and sword.
"THE BUCKTAIL REGIMENT," they were called, their honor they upheld,
Through many blood-stained battle fields where they faced shot and shell,
They never knew the word retreat, or quailed at death's arms,
The Union's trust was in them placed, defended by their arms.
Mechanicsville and Malvern Hill, Bull Run and Fredericksburg,
Antietam and South Mountain too, their battle cry was heard,
Gaines Mill and Groveton, Gettysburg, The Wilderness also,

New Market Cross Roads, where brave blood in rivulets did flow.
Catlett's Station was the same, and yet Bethesda church
Where death did stock in bullets form, for soldiers' lives to search,
The Bucktail Regiment never flinched, 'twas always in the van,
The mountain men stood side by side to save their "Yankee Land."
We raise this monument today to those who've gone before,
And they who have been spared to us, we warmly greet once more.
All honor to the Bucktails; their names will never die.
May they receive all blessings here, and eternal peace on high.

—John F. Sullivan[282]

This poem, published in 1908 about the Bucktail Regiment of the Civil War, was a prelude to the dedication of a marker to this famous regiment in Driftwood, located "near the intersection of Bennetts Branch and Driftwood streams, the spot agreed upon being at or near the embarkation of General Kane's Bucktails."[283]

At the time of the firing on Fort Sumter, April 12, 1861, Thomas L. Kane was involved in building a home in the Pennsylvania Wilds for his family at present-day Kane, Pennsylvania. The son of a federal judge from Philadelphia, Kane had come into the region to visit lands owned by his father.

Kane had worked in Philadelphia as a law clerk and lawyer but was a reformer at heart and interested himself in religious liberty and women's rights, battled against poverty in Philadelphia and founded and financed a school for Philadelphia's poor children.[284] Kane was also an abolitionist, a man who lived what he believed, hiding slaves on the second floor of his father's stable. "Judge Kane felt that his son was not faithfully obeying the law. Finally, he had him held in contempt of court and thrown into prison."[285] Fortunately for Kane, Robert C. Grier, an associate justice of the U.S. Supreme Court, overruled Judge Kane's conviction.[286]

Local newspapers carried messages from Pennsylvania governor Curtin:

The War Begun
Bombardment of Fort Sumter
16 HOURS' FIGHTING

THE UNCONDITIONAL SURRENDER
OF FORT SUMTER FULLY CONFIRMED

The President Calls for 75,000 Militia[287]

Brig. Gen. THOMAS L. KANE.

PUBLISHED BY
McALLISTER & BRO. 728 Chestnut Street, Philada.

Thomas L. Kane. *Library of Congress.*

Kane immediately took action, contacting Governor Curtin asking for permission to recruit a company of volunteer riflemen from among the hardy woodsmen of McKean County, which grew to include men from Elk, Cameron, Tioga, Warren, Clearfield, Perry, Carbon and Chester Counties.[288]

The name Bucktail Regiment came when Kane noticed one of the volunteers cross the street from his headquarters in Smethport to a butcher shop that was processing venison, where the recruit pulled out his penknife, cut off the tail of a deer and stuck it in his cap. And so the idea for their unique uniforms was born. Kane noted,

> *It was not in my power to procure uniforms. But red flannel for shirts was obtainable in quantity at the country shops, and felt hats. Bucktails, too, lie about our cabins by the dozen. Each volunteer was made to mount one of them in imitation of my own, and was directed to have faith that he would one day be prouder of it than any ostrich plume.*[289]

The movement gained momentum. With the assistance of William T. Blanchard, a railroad construction worker, the McKean County Rifles was formed. "On April 23, 1861, at nine o'clock in the morning, the command 'Forward march' was given, and the men headed across the mountains to Cameron County. There they met John Eldred, the newly elected Cameron County sheriff, who formed the Cameron County Rifles. On April 24, the two companies were joined by the Elk County Rifles, headed by volunteer Thomas B. Winslow from Benezette, and nephew of its founder, Reuben Colburn Winslow, as well as a few men from Tioga County."[290]

On April 27, after two days of work building four rafts of rough pine boards, 16 feet long by 10 or 12 inches wide by 7/8 inches thick, the men were ready to set off in the Sinnemahoning Creek to begin the journey to Harrisburg. A special platform had been built for Colonel Kane's horse, Old Glencoe, and the Stars and Stripes was flying high from a green hickory pole with a bucktail attached for a flagstaff. One could hear the strains of a fife and the beat of drums echoing through the forest as they began their journey.[291]

The trip was not an easy one.

> *The river below the Sinnemahoning Creek passes through gorges and canyons, and is honeycombed with rapids, the current at many places attaining a speed of ten miles an hour....The swiftness of the current and the rocks and rapids of the river, made the journey a memorable*

Thomas B. Winslow. *Library of Congress.*

one. Despite the experience of the steersmen and their knowledge of raftsmanship, time and time again the heavily loaded rafts grounded on rocks, compelling the men to slip overboard into the cold water and by sheer strength lift the rafts over the obstructions. Toward sunset, some four miles above Rattlesnake Falls, in deep water, the four rafts were massed together and the Bucktails, though soaked to the skin, thankful that they had succeeded in shooting the rapids, celebrated the event by singing with all their power the "Star Spangled Banner." At Rattlesnake Falls a stop was made for the night, the people of the place doing everything within their power to provide shelter. The next morning the Bucktails were carried on the railroad to Lock Haven.[292]

And then on to Harrisburg to join the other forces from Pennsylvania.

Over 350,000 Pennsylvanians served in the Union army, more than from any other Northern state except for New York, and the Bucktail Regiment is considered to be Pennsylvania's most famous Civil War unit.[293]

As one surveys the monument and Sinnemahoning Creek beyond, consider that the local men of the Benezette region who joined the Bucktails were volunteers and served their country well.

ABOLITIONISTS

As mentioned in the chapter about the founding of Benezette and being named for abolitionist Anthony Benezet by Reuben Winslow, who also had ties to the Underground Railroad, Thomas Kane, founder of the Bucktails, was a Philadelphia abolitionist. It is possible that he knew Reuben Winslow before the outbreak of the Civil War through the lumber trade and influenced the naming of Benezette.

A local historian, Raymond Nelson, has pointed out that people within the Benezette region had ties to Philadelphia and the abolitionists who were active there. Prior to the Civil War, a number of wealthy Philadelphians bought land in the Keating area twenty-five miles east of Benezette in Clinton County. One of those was Stephen Girard (1750–1831), who owned over 6,000 acres in central Pennsylvania. Girard had endowed Girard College and, at his death, willed some of the land to the City of Philadelphia. Nelson claims to have examined a deed that transferred land from the city to escaped slaves, a number of whom had established themselves in the Keating area. In 1802, Thew Johnson, an English Quaker, arrived in Philadelphia, where he lived for several years. He and his wife eventually came into what was then Gibson Township, Clearfield County, now Cameron County. During his time in Philadelphia, he became acquainted with the abolitionist movement. In 1849, Johnson bought 999 acres (warrant no. 5023) for $350 in Elk County, where he located the village of Grant, three miles downstream from Benezette. The historian further noted that Benezette Township in Elk County shares a common border with Girard Township in Clearfield County, which is only eight miles from Rush Township in Centre County. Rush Township was named "as a tribute of respect to the memory of the truly venerable and supereminent Dr. Benjamin Rush." Rush, Girard and Anthony Benezet all lived in Philadelphia about the same time.[294] As outlined in an earlier book by this author, *The Pennsylvania Wilds and the Civil War*, each of the twelve and a half counties in the Wilds was active in the Underground Railroad movement. As it was illegal, per the Fugitive Slave Act, to harbor runaway slaves, information about who was involved and how was kept secret. The details of the purchase of land in Keating and the naming of townships after abolitionists or those having ties to Philadelphia suggest that there may have been extensive local involvement in the movement, but that involvement remains hidden.

Chapter 8

CONSERVATION

The Civilian Conservation Corps (CCC)

The Civilian Conservation Corps was a work relief program established by executive order on April 5, 1933, that provided millions of young men employment during the Great Depression. It is considered one of the most successful of President Franklin Roosevelt's New Deal programs. The work of the Civilian Conservation Corps was to plant trees and construct trails and shelters.[295] What better area to do that work than in the Pennsylvania Wilds?

Locally, camps were established at Hicks Run (May 30, 1933–October 10, 1935), Dents Run (June 20, 1933–1938), Sinnemahoning (July 10, 1933–1941), Medix Run (June 11, 1933–1941) and Caledonia (June 21, 1933–January 1939).

The son of one of those workers left his testimony about his father's work at Camp S-131-PA, located at Hicks Run and officially known as Potterdale:

> *My father, J. Fred Ledger, Jr. of Bridgeport, Pennsylvania, was born on October 20, 1913. He was the fourth child in a family with four boys and one girl. The family lived along the Schuylkill Canal and later moved to another house in Bridgeport. He was 19 years old when he joined the Civilian Conservation Corps. After training, he reported to Camp S-131 at Hicks Run, Pennsylvania, in 1933. At the time, he was dating my mother-to-be who was still in high school in Norristown, Pennsylvania. They corresponded every week, sometimes more than once. There were some*

CCC Camp S-131 - 1933
Hicks Run, PA

This page: Hicks Run
Civilian Conservation
Camp. *Pennsylvania
Department of Conservation
and Natural Resources.*

*other local men at the camp and one, Tom Quinn, was best man at my
parents wedding in 1935. Dad had been a Boy Scout and spent a lot
of time fishing and hunting along the Schuylkill River and didn't mind
the rough conditions experienced in the mountains of Pennsylvania. He
said conditions were primitive and the work hard, but it was the Great
Depression and the men were happy to have a job. The CCC was clearing
land and building roads. The men slept on cots low to the ground in large
tents, shaking their boots out each morning to be sure no snakes were in
them. There were a lot of snakes. He sent rattles from a timber rattlesnake
in one of his letters to my mother, and once told me that one of the guys
was bitten on the hand by a non-poisonous black snake. The bite became
infected. There were only occasional visits by a dentist with the patients
sitting on a peach basket for treatment.[296]*

Many of the recruits came to the camps hungry and poorly clothed. They were issued uniforms and given three meals a day and earned thirty dollars a month. Many of the men sent the money home to their families to help offset the effects of the Great Depression.[297]

While the army ran the camps, foresters, carpenters and other civilians directed the work. The work of the men included fighting forest fires, planting trees and building roads, buildings, picnic areas, swimming areas and campgrounds. The CCC created many state parks.[298]

Pennsylvania had the second-highest number of camps, 151, second only to California. Due to the forward thinking of Governor Gifford Pinchot, Pennsylvania received so many camps because the commonwealth already had a plan in place for them. A total of 194,500 Pennsylvanians served in the CCC program nationwide. The CCC added greatly to the Pennsylvania Bureau of State Parks. The program ended on June 30, 1942, due to the outbreak of World War II.[299]

THE QUEHANNA WILD AREA

Nearly 50,000 acres, the Quehanna Wild area is a protected wildlife area, home to several species of birds and other animals including elk, deer and coyotes.[300]

Its History

The 1950s brought about change to a large area of land located in Elk, Cameron and Clearfield Counties today known as the Quehanna Wild Area.

The change began with the presidency of Dwight Eisenhower. The old warrior was

determined to solve "the fearful atomic dilemma" by finding some way by which "the miraculous inventiveness of man" would not be dedicated to his death, but consecrated to his life. In his Atoms for Peace speech before the United Nations General Assembly on December 8, 1953, President Eisenhower sought to solve this terrible problem by suggesting a means to transform the atom from a scourge into a benefit for mankind.[301]

Quehanna Wild Area sign. *Nicholas Tonelli at visitPA.com.*

The result of his proposal was that many programs were developed for the peaceful use of atomic energy.

One company interested in the use of atomic energy was the Curtiss-Wright Company. In 1929, Curtiss-Wright was formed by a merger of two companies, one founded by Glenn Curtiss, the father of naval aviation, and the other by the Wright brothers, who made the first flight.[302] By 1955, Curtiss-Wright, which was planning to develop and test nuclear-powered jet engines, was looking for a remote location to construct a research center. The Quehanna Wild Area presented the remoteness the company was seeking.

In the 1870s, the Pennsylvania timber industry was not interested in conservation but rather in taking the best trees, leaving areas covered with unwanted logs, branches and broken timber. "Once rich forests of white pine, beech and hemlock had become what University of Pennsylvania botany professor, Joseph Rothrock, was calling 'the Pennsylvania Desert.'"[303]

Recognizing the need for strong forest management, thanks in part to Rothrock's lectures and writings, in 1895, the commonwealth appointed him the first forest commissioner in what was known as the Pennsylvania Department of Forests and Waters, today's Department of Conservation and Natural Recources (DCNR). Rothrock urged the creation of publicly owned forest reserves to protect the forests from what he described as "humanity's tree-destroying instinct."[304] Logging companies were happy to receive five dollars an acre for cutover land from the commonwealth. By the time Rothrock retired, more than 443,000 acres of forest had been acquired for use as public lands.[305]

Locally, in 1898, the state bought land that became Moshannon State Forest. In 1900, its second purchase was made: 3,263 acres in the Quehanna region. Elk State Forest was purchased in 1900. Combining these regions, 46 percent of the Quehanna Wild Area lies in the Elk State Forest, with the remainder in the Moshannon State Forest.[306]

In 1955, Curtiss-Wright purchased nine thousand acres of remote land in the region, leasing an additional forty-two thousand acres. This land included four hundred acres (one-fifth of the leased lands) in Benezette Township.[307]

The governor of Pennsylvania, George Leader, signed legislation that authorized the construction of a research facility at Quehanna. The land was sold to Curtiss-Wright for $22.50 an acre, and the company was also given a ninety-nine-year lease on the remaining 42,596 acres. The state constructed $1.6 million of roads in the area. The Quehanna Highway was built on parts of an old CCC road that followed an earlier logging railroad grade. The state cancelled 212 camp leases out of concerns about the security of the research that was to take place there. Construction on the site included a nuclear research center with a nuclear reactor and six shielded radiation containment chambers; a place for jet engine trials with two test cells and bunkers; and an industrial complex where Curon foam for furniture and household products was manufactured.[308]

The name Quehanna was adopted by Curtiss-Wright, from the Susquehanna River. The nearby West Branch of the Susquehanna was the route traveled by both Native Americans and early settlers into the region.

There are various accounts of how the river acquired that name, one attributed to a conversation that was overheard.

> *The word, Susquehanna, properly Sisquehanna, from Sisku, "mud" and hanne, "a stream," was probably at an early time of the settling of this country overheard by someone while the Indians were at the time of a flood or freshet ["a great rise or overflowing of a stream caused by heavy rain or melted snow"] remarking, "Juh Achsis quehanne," which is "How muddy the stream is," and therefore taken as the proper name of the river.[309]*

The name may also reference the Native Americans who were early inhabitants of Pennsylvania, the Susquehannocks, who controlled the drainage area of both the North and West Branches of the Susquehanna River.[310]

The Curtiss-Wright project created excitement in the region, with the potential for six thousand jobs. A total of $20 million was spent erecting plants, homes, offices, utility facilities and related items. Locally, a road was constructed from Medix Run to the site. A new post office was established.[311]

Curtiss-Wright offered special training and subsequent employment for young men at the new Research and Development Center.

> *According to an announcement issued jointly by Curtiss-Wright and The Pennsylvania State University…a special group of 25 young men is to be recruited from the area for a 27 week training program at the Research and Development Center in drafting and design. Those completing the program successfully will be hired immediately by Curtiss-Wright for work at Quehanna. Penn State is cooperating with Curtiss-Wright on the project in two principal areas: the screening and selection of applicants, and, providing the actual instruction. The teaching staff will consist of members of the Penn State Faculty who will be assigned fulltime to Quehanna.…The courses of instruction have been developed by the College of Engineering and Architecture at Penn State.[312]*

By 1960, the air force had decided not to pursue nuclear-powered aircraft, and the federal government cancelled $70 million in high-altitude testing contracts with Curtiss-Wright.[313] That was the beginning of the end for the Quehanna project. Eventually, Curtiss-Wright turned over the leased land

Earth mound over jet engine test bunker in Quehanna Wild Area, Cameron County, Pennsylvania. *Ruhrfisch (talk), Wikimedia Commons.*

An opening in one of the bunkers, Quehanna Wild Area. *Wikimedia Commons.*

to the commonwealth and Pennsylvania reacquired all the acreage that had been sold to Curtiss-Wright. By November 1967, all the land had been turned back to state forests and state game lands.[314] Today, a few remaining bunkers are visible, gradually being overtaken by the wilds.

In 1970, the name of the state's largest wild area, fifty thousand acres, was officially changed to the Quehanna Wild Area. A seventy-five-mile Quehanna Trail System has been built through the wild area and surrounding state forests. While no permanent residents are allowed, primitive camping by hikers is permitted. Quehanna Wild Area has been named an Important Bird Area by the Pennsylvania Audubon Society and is home to many species of birds and animals including elk, coyote and other game.[315]

Marion E. Brooks Natural Area

Local outdoor writer Jim Ross grew up on the Ross homestead in Medix Run, and on a beautiful day was fishing the little stream of Medix Run which flows past his home. He had just rounded the bend when he came upon a woman who was casting expertly into the best fishing hole in the

Marion E. Brooks Natural Area marker, Moshannon State Forest, Elk County, Pennsylvania. *Wikimedia Commons.*

stream. The occasion marked the first time Ross set eyes on the woman who showed abundant energy. The two met in 1945 and since then the outspoken Marion Brooks has gained the reputation as the foremost conservationist for the entire Northwestern Pennsylvania.[316]

Marion Brooks was born in Allegheny County, Pennsylvania, and arrived in Medix Run when she bought property below Haystack Mountain. Her concern for hunter safety around her home inspired her to form the Bennetts Valley Ambulance Association and serve as a civil defense policewoman. Her concerns about preventing water pollution from strip mine drainage led to the establishment of the Toby Valley Watershed Association.[317] She was a prime mover in organizing the Medix Run Sportsmen's Club and a donor of land to the club, a delegate to the Elk County Federation of Sportsmen's

Clubs, chairman of the State Federation's Fish Committee, the first woman to head the North Central District as president and organizer of the Toby Valley and Bennett's Valley Watershed Associations. Before her death in 1973, she had been named Conservationist of the Year by the Pennsylvania Forestry Association and presented with the Pennsylvania Fish Commission's White Hat award in 1972.[318]

Known for her brash language and outspokeness, Marion was also a caring person. She once worked with a doctor who had a drinking problem and had been forced out of practice. She got him back on his feet and into the practice of healing once again. On another occasion, a man died on a hunting trip somewhere in the forests near Quehanna. Through waist-deep snow, Marion finally found him, after several tiring trips, when others couldn't. She refused the $1,000 reward offered for locating his body.[319]

Because of Marion's determination, more people got involved in conservation, including the Boy Scouts. She worked closely with them, aiding them on their annual browse-cutting projects.[320] The Allegheny Trails Council of Boy Scouts from Pittsburgh came to lend a hand as well; in 1974, about four hundred Scouts in the Medix Run area staying in tents took part in the project.[321]

In 1975, the plaque designating the Marion E. Brooks Natural Area was dedicated. It was constructed of white cement with natural rocks imbedded in it, and the bronze plaque reads: "Marion E. Brooks Natural Area…These 975 acres of white birch are dedicated to Marion E. Brooks and her lifetime of devotion to preserving the natural beauty of our forests and streams… 'Someone who cared'…Born 1912…Died 1973."[322]

The tract of white birch, part of the Moshannon State Forest, is said to be the southernmost stand of white birch in this section of the state.[323]

Beaver Run Dam Wildlife Viewing Area

The access to Beaver Run Dam Wildlife Viewing Area is found near the intersection of Quehanna Highway and Beaver Run Road. Shallow water impoundments offer opportunities to view waterfowl, wading birds, deer and songbirds. In open fields nearby, one can catch an occasional glimpse of elk, white-tailed deer and wild turkey.[324] Approximately 350 yards from the parking lot down a flat, forested trail, a viewing blind has been built from which you can take in the wildlife, including nesting osprey in the spring.[325]

Wildlife viewing blind at Beaver Dam Run Wildlife Viewing Area in Quehanna Wild Area.
Ruhrfisch (talk), Wikimedia Commons.

Teaberry Loop Trail Vista

The Teaberry Loop Trail Vista is located approximately 330 yards from an unmarked pull-off along the Quehanna Highway. A well-worn trail leads from the pull-off to a vista overlooking the Paige Run and Red Run Valleys.[326] The trail, approximately four miles long, is described as moderately difficult, with some sections difficult due to the steep grade. According to DCNR, the trail is marked with blue blazes.[327]

Table Falls

Access to Table Falls can be found a few yards away from a marked parking area along Red Run Road. Follow the trail from the back of the parking area downhill, and Table Falls is approximately fifty yards downstream. The best time to view the falls is during high water, which generally is in springtime after the thaw, or during times of heavy rain.[328]

Teaberry Loop Trail: vista of the Paige Run and Red Run drainage area, Elk County, Pennsylvania, within Moshannon State Forest. *Wikimedia Commons.*

Table Falls on Paige Run. *Pennsylvania Great Outdoors Visitors Bureau.*

Wykoff Run Falls, Elk State Forest, Cameron County, Pennsylvania. *Nicholas, Wikimedia Commons.*

Wykoff Run Falls

Wykoff Run Falls is located along the Wykoff Road, which is approximately halfway between the Quehanna Highway and the village of Sinnemahoning. The best time to visit Wykoff Run Falls is following the spring thaw or times of heavy rain.[329] Wykoff Run Road is known as one of the top motorcycle drives in Pennsylvania, featuring sweeps and turns as it follows a clear mountain stream with pull-off areas for riders.[330]

Chapter 9

ELK HERD

A New Industry Is Born: Tourism

The Benezette region has seen many changes over the years from various industries: logging, coal and a gas boom. Each era impacted the people and the land. As these industries waned, the Benezette region's population did not grow. Its residents were forced to find employment in other industries, such as the powder metal industry in nearby St. Marys, Pennsylvania.

What the region did have was a wild elk herd that the Pennsylvania Game Commission had been overseeing since 1912.

It was former Pennsylvania governor Ed Rendell who had a new vision for the region. "He was raised in Manhattan and was the mayor of Philadelphia, so how ironic is that? He saw what others probably couldn't see. He made the stars align," said Rawley Cogan, president, CEO and cofounder of the Keystone Elk Country Alliance, in an interview with the *Philadelphia Inquirer* in March 2021.[331] According to the article, the commonwealth invested $6 million in the property, a former Christmas tree farm, and the alliance came up with an additional $6 million through fundraising. "Rendell said seeing elk for the first time made the visitors center an easy sell. I mean, they're unbelievable. They market themselves."[332] That was the vision that led to the construction of the Elk Country Visitor Center and various other buildings on the property and the setting aside of lands for elk viewing that has turned the Benezette region into a major tourist attraction.

Elk Country Visitor Center, Winslow Hill, Benezette, Pennsylvania. *John Myers.*

Elk Expo, Great Room, Elk Country Visitor Center, July 29, 2023. *John Myers.*

Elk Expo, Discovery Room, Elk Country Visitor Center, July 29, 2023. *John Myers.*

Cogan noted that in 2019, the visitor center's recorded attendance was 520,000 people. In 2020, during the COVID-19 pandemic, with the center closed for two months, 518,000 people visited.[333]

FRED JR., BULL NO. 36

He was a welcoming presence in the village—a goodwill ambassador of sorts. May Freddy's spirit forever rest on the village of Benezette and Winslow Hill.[334]

He has been called Pennsylvania's most famous elk, Fred, Fred Jr., Freddy or Bull No. 36—the name attached to him by the Pennsylvania Game Commission for the numbered radio collar he wore. For our purposes, he is Fred.

Fred has been the subject of blog posts by wildlife photographers and was recognized by many residents of the region over the years. He is displayed on bottles of a sweet red wine produced by Laurel Mountain Winery and sold at Benezette Wines called Old Fred #36. One writer who had followed him over a period of years wrote on his death, "Native Americans believe that elk are spirit animals. They symbolize strength, endurance and perseverance. Members of the Lakota tribe of the Sioux nation have always considered Wapiti sacred. This bull elk was all that, and then some."[335] Many biologists believe the name Wapiti is a Shawnee Indian word meaning "white rump," an appropriate description of the elk's large rump patch.[336]

Pennsylvania wildlife photographer Willard Hill, whose photographs accompany this chapter, first encountered Fred in 1997. He describes an occasion when he came across several mature bulls chasing a cow during the rut on Winslow Hill. At that time, Fred, being a young bull, was around the edge of the action.[337] The bulls have to earn their "harem" of cows, so to speak. Hill encountered Fred again in 1998, when he described Fred as a "satellite" bull while a more mature bull was with the herd. Hill notes that Fred defeated that bull in a lengthy fight in 2001.[338]

According to the Pennsylvania Game Commission,

Each year a bull grows large branching antlers that sweep up and back from the head. In May, two bumps start to swell on the skull, pushing up about half an inch per day. The growing antlers are covered with a soft skin called velvet. This covering contains blood vessels which supply growth materials to the enlarging antlers.…Before the autumn rutting season, the velvet dries and is shed or rubbed off. Bulls carry their antlers into late winter or early spring.[339]

The mating season is September and October. Bulls bugle to attract cows, and they fight with other bulls to become, or maintain the position of, supreme bull. The battles seem intense, with the bulls locking horns, pushing and shoving each other. Generally, there is no serious injury, and the weaker bull pulls away. A bull elk may have a harem of fifteen to twenty cows. The younger bulls that hang around the edge of the herd may also share in breeding.[340]

The game commission regularly cautions observers that elk are wild animals, much larger and heavier than the white-tailed deer that inhabit the region. A mature elk is fifty to sixty inches at the shoulder, weighing six hundred to one thousand pounds. Females weigh between five hundred and six hundred pounds.[341]

Fred Jr., 2004. *Willard C. Hill.*

There are various estimates of Fred's age; some speculate that he was twenty years old when he died in 2011, which would have made his birth year 1991. An analysis of his rack size in 1997 and 1998 seems to point to him having been born no later than 1994, also noting the possibility that he could have been born as early as 1992.[342]

Fred Jr. bugling, 2005. *Willard C. Hill.*

While studies show that bull elk rarely live beyond age twelve, Pennsylvania elk have a longer life than elk in the western states because of plentiful habitat, few predators, lower elevations and less severe winters.[343]

In an interview with the *Williamsport Sun-Gazette*, one woman who had a home in Benezette and visited every weekend noted that while most elk wander around, "We always look for Fred when we come in on Friday nights. He hardly ever leaves town."[344] She said Fred chose to stay near humans. He was in her yard so frequently that a friend made a sign reading, "Fred's Woods."[345] Fred was so popular that people would drive by asking if she had seen Fred or where he was hanging out that day. "It is not unusual to find calves and cows near cars in the driveway and bulls bedded down in the yard."[346]

While Fred seemed to prefer living in Benezette, he returned to Winslow Hill each fall to breed. One of the most photographed wild elk in the region, he won many rut fights competing against other bulls.[347]

Above: Fred Jr. sleeping, the last year he was alive. *Willard C. Hill.*

Left: Old Fred #36, Mountain Laurel Winery at Benezette Wines. *John Myers.*

In his declining years, Fred's arthritic knees made movement difficult, and he was blind in one eye. His antlers' size had diminished. Living through a tough winter, in January 2011, at the estimated age of nineteen, Fred suffered some injuries on the ice and was in distress with a broken leg and possibly a broken pelvis. He was unable to get back up. Noting there was no way he could recover, the game commission euthanized him.[348]

In the final autumn of his life, he managed to make the trek to Winslow Hill and breed, adding to an undetermined number of offspring.[349] Will one of them someday become another Fred?

Restoration of the Elk Herd
into the Pennsylvania Wilds

The history of the restoration of the elk herd into the Pennsylvania Wilds is a remarkable story. Eastern elk once roamed the commonwealth of Pennsylvania, with vast herds found from northern New York to central Georgia. Pennsylvania's largest concentration of elk was believed to have been in the Allegheny Mountains. Colonization led to their demise, as elk were pursued wherever they were found.[350]

By the mid-1860s, a few native elk were still roaming in Pennsylvania's Elk and Cameron Counties. Gone were the vast herds that trampled the ground around the naturally occurring salt licks in their "quest to lick the salt."[351] By the end of that decade, the last elk had been killed in Elk County.

The Pennsylvania Game Commission was established in 1895. In 1912, Joseph Kalbfus, the agency's secretary, spoke about the possibility of reintroducing elk in Pennsylvania. The elk herds in Yellowstone National Park and the Jackson Hole Refuge Area had increased to the point that the biologists who were responsible for protecting the remnants of the elk population had come up with a plan to relocate some of the herd while trying to feed the remaining elk through the winter months. In 1913, Pennsylvania received its first shipment of Yellowstone elk by train. The fifty elk cost about thirty dollars each. Half of them went to Clinton County, the other half to Clearfield County. Later in the year, twenty-two elk were brought in and released on state lands in Monroe County; the remainder were released at a Centre County preserve.[352]

The elk were brought into the region by boxcar and chased into the Wilds, a terrain much different than the one they knew in Yellowstone. According to the game commission, when the elk were released, they began to wander in search of food and cover, and "within a week, some had traveled as far as forty miles away from the release sites."[353]

While many people were in favor of the elk program, the animals were destructive in farming areas. Illegal harvests by poachers and farmers, as well as those who wanted to hunt them, were not uncommon.

Fred's ancestors also had to adjust to the climate, and there were some early deaths among the herd. According to a 1913 newspaper article reporting on the loss of some of the Yellowstone elk,

> *Used to high altitudes in the cold, dry air, they were not acclimated to the moist atmosphere of Pennsylvania; consequently, they were very*

138

susceptible to pulmonary disease....The State Game Commission has hopes of saving the others, and they are being very carefully looked after by the game warden.[354]

In 1913, the Pennsylvania General Assembly enacted a law protecting the elk until November 1921, when a two-week elk season would be held. Bulls with at least four points to one antler were identified in the law as legal game for the distant season.[355]

In 1970, a news article in the *Progress* stated that the elk became so abundant from 1923 to 1932 that an open season was held to hunt them. Since that time, the elk have been protected. According to that same 1970 article, a ten-point program was developed for consideration by state agencies. Noting that the elk range encompassed about 10,560 acres owned by the game commission and various other organizations, it was proposed in the ten-point program that all the land in question could be acquired by direct purchase or exchange by the game commission.[356]

Today's visitors to the region are seeing firsthand the results of the combined efforts of the Pennsylvania Game Commission, the Pennsylvania Department of Conservation and Natural Resources, the Keystone Elk Country Alliance and other organizations to protect the elk and their habitat.[357] It is estimated that 1,400 elk living in Pennsylvania are descendants of the Yellowstone elk.[358]

According to information in a five-year elk management plan (2020–25) adopted by the Pennsylvania Game Commission, in 1970, interest in the elk herd began to rise. Pennsylvania State University (PSU) began a research study with help from the Game Commission; the Department of Forests and Waters, which became the Department of Conservation and Natural Resources (DCNR); and the Northcentral Pennsylvania Economic Development District. The study was designed to evaluate ecology, population dynamics and movements of the Pennsylvania elk herd. A graduate student spent the autumn months counting and recounting elk, by foot and from a vehicle. His estimate of the overall elk population the year he counted was around sixty-five, give or take three. From 1972 to 1974, Penn State graduate students continued the counts and determined there was a steady decline in population. When the Penn State research concluded in 1974, the Pennsylvania Game Commission and DCNR completed ground surveys, and in 1975, they estimated the elk population had dropped to its lowest level ever, with an estimated twenty-eight to thirty-three elk. Surveys continued over the years using various methods, including observations recorded by helicopter. In late 1981, the game commission began marking elk with radio collars to assist in the annual survey.[359]

While it was alarming to read that the elk herd had dropped to such low numbers, plans were devised to disk and seed old logging and access roads. Timber was removed in areas to provide browse, and several old fields and clear-cuts were disked, limed, fertilized and planted with a mixture of grasses.[360]

In 2001, the Elk Habitat Challenge Initiative was launched. A partnership between the Pennsylvania Game Commission, DCNR/Bureau of Forests and the Rocky Mountain Elk Foundation set out to raise $1.2 million in public and private funds to improve elk habitat. The response to the three-year initiative was overwhelming: twelve different private organizations and companies, along with the Rocky Mountain Elk Foundation and the state agencies, answered the call. Over $830,000 was raised for habitat development (food plots) of 593 acres, including lime and fertilizer. Equipment was purchased, and other small acreages were improved. The Pennsylvania Game Commission continues to increase food plots on public lands, many of which are located at mine reclamation sites.[361]

According to the statistics presented in the elk management habitat plan, 3,750 square miles is under management. The management areas are mowed at least once a year during the growing season and receive lime and fertilizer on a three- to five-year rotation.[362]

It takes dedicated maintenance personnel working to maintain these food plots. Taking into account the recent estimate, 1,400 from a low point of 28 to 33 in 1975 is an incredible turnaround in the elk herd. The management of the herd is not just planning and growing food plots. Birthing patterns, health issues and deaths are also studied.

As this book was being written, on September 29, 2023, a local television station carried a story on its website about a "6x6" bull elk in Sinnemahoning whose antlers were entangled in telephone wire. Photos show a dish from a satellite receiver and wire lying on the ground. To free the elk, he was sedated as his rescuers worked to cut the wire from his antlers. The bull walked away unharmed, and the game commission fitted him with a GPS tracking device to monitor his future health.[363]

In 2001, elk hunting was reintroduced in Pennsylvania after an absence of almost seventy years. It is a controlled hunt with a specific number of male and female elk licenses awarded to hunters via a lottery system that takes place at the Elk Country Visitor Center. The 2023 drawing was held in the month of July.

"Game Commission Rescues Elk Trapped in Telephone Wire," *WTAJ* (Johnstown, PA), September 29, 2023. *Pennsylvania Game Commission.*

Since 1975, records have been kept of known elk deaths and their causes. Some deaths resulted from farmers killing the elk for crop damage, some from illegal poaching and some from vehicle collisions. In the most recent ten-year period, deaths due to elk/vehicle collisions have exceeded those due to both crop damage and poaching, with the game commission noting that outside of the legal harvest of elk, vehicle collisions cause the greatest number of deaths in the elk herd.[364]

A word of caution to those traveling the roads in the elk range: drive with a watchful eye and be aware that elk and deer may be crossing the highways. Watching your driving speed is also important!

Chapter 10

THE ROAD TO MT. ZION

The word *Zion* comes from the Hebrew word *tsiyon*, meaning "hill."[365] References to Zion and Mt. Zion are found throughout the Old and New Testaments of the Bible. The name Mt. Zion was given to the first Protestant church in Elk County, which sat on a wooded hill above the village of Caledonia.

Along the road to Mt. Zion, which is very near Benezette, are four special places where people can meditate, relax, reflect on the history of the region or simply take in the beauty of the scenery that surrounds them. Three are relatively new locations; the fourth, an active historic cemetery, received its first "resident" in 1838.

All these sites are easy to discover. Heading to Benezette from Medix Run, just before entering Benezette, there is a road leading off Route 555, Gray Hill Road. Turning left on Gray Hill Road for about 2.6 miles leads one to an intersection with Rock Hill Road. A sign there indicates a left turn on Rock Hill Road, which leads to the Little Chapel in the Woods.

Also from Gray Hill Road, very near the Rock Hill Road intersection, one can pick up Mt. Zion Road. Following Mt. Zion Road, the Cross on the Hill is located off the right side of the road. Continuing past the Cross on the Hill on Mt. Zion Road leads one to Mt. Zion Cemetery and the Mt. Zion Historic Park.

THE LITTLE CHAPEL IN THE WOODS

The Little Chapel in the Woods is a recent addition to the landscape of the Benezette region. Its formal title is the Fred Bartholme Memorial Chapel, and it was built in memory of Fred Bartholme by his son, John. John and his wife, Liz, are the owners of Medix Run Lodges, and the chapel is built on the lodges' grounds. Nearby is the Kincaid Family Cemetery, the resting place of Lydia Kincaid, wife of Dr. Noah Kincaid, both early settlers, who are remembered in the chapter on Caledonia.

The chapel, overlooking the Buttermilk Run Valley, is easy to find traveling on Rock Hill Road. Its copper roof catches the eye of those pausing to look at this beautiful building. Construction of the chapel began in July 2020 and was completed by April 2021. The chapel has a wraparound deck. An eleven-foot cross is located in a grassy spot behind the building. A walk to the cross reveals the valley below.

Beyond the beauty of the setting and building itself is the beauty in the story of its creation. The Fred Bartholme Memorial Chapel was built in memory of the man who frequently brought his son, John, who grew up in

The Fred Bartholme Memorial Chapel (the Little Chapel in the Woods). *John Myers.*

Kincaid Family Cemetery located near the Little Chapel in the Woods. *John Myers.*

Franklin, Pennsylvania, to the region, exploring the valley and mountains as a child. The family owned a camp in nearby Cameron County for more than fifty years.

In an interview with John Bartholme, it stood out that he had an attachment to the area because of those childhood trips. His wife, from Alaska, was also taken with the region, and eventually they returned to the area and became owners of the property in 2003. The Medix Run Lodges and Chapel are situated on seventy acres. John's father visited John and Liz there and pitched in to help with the wood cutting and general help necessary to maintain the grounds.

Through the years, Fred faced many health challenges. In 2020, he passed away from Alzheimer's and Parkinson's disease. Prior to Fred's death, John told his dad of his plan to memorialize him by building the chapel in his honor. And Fred, even with his diminished faculties, said, "As long as I get the best seat in the house." Fred did, in fact, get the best seat in the house. He is enshrined in the chapel overlooking the beautiful valley.

Additionally, there are many personal touches provided by family and friends: the interior walls of the chapel are made from hand-hewn native white pine. Backless wooden benches and a 350-pound wooden altar were created by local artisan Dave McCloskey, and a beautiful stained-glass window was created by Bartholme's two aunts. Friends donated an antique bell, which hangs by the entrance.[366]

With the chapel completed in April 2021, a celebration was held for its opening, with family and friends from Franklin and elsewhere attending. The lives of not only Fred Bartholme but also others who had been lost in the COVID pandemic were celebrated and remembered.

In this peaceful setting, nondenominational services by lay ministers are held every three to four weeks.[367]

THE CROSS ON THE HILL

Approximately 2.7 miles from Route 555, Gray Hill Road turns into Mt. Zion Road. After 3.3 miles, you'll see the Cross on the Hill Interfaith Memorial on the right, overlooking the Spring Run Valley.[368]

On a sunny August day in 2023, the author and her husband were searching for the Cross on the Hill. Easily finding the location and pulling into the parking lot, they noticed three parked motorcycles. Exiting their vehicle, as they walked up to the cross a short distance away, they passed artwork that depicted scenes from the Bible and the life of Christ, cut of iron. These pieces were created by inmates at Fort Leavenworth, Kansas.[369]

Approaching the cross, one can gaze across beautiful Spring Run Valley. The cross itself is an impressive marker at thirteen feet tall and eight feet across. "Erected in 1990, the cross was envisioned as an interfaith memorial and a place for meditation and spiritual healing."[370]

Three motorcycles led to three people sitting on various benches placed near the cross. Striking up a conversation, the author and her husband learned that the three were from the state of Michigan, living near Detroit. One of the three observed that he had never known of a place that was so peaceful and quiet as what they were experiencing at the cross. They had come to the region to see the elk and been directed to the cross.

Questions about the cross and the development of the area surrounding it led to a conversation between the author and one of its organizers and its present caretaker, Bill McMahon of DuBois. McMahon is a retired mail carrier, and the Benezette region was his route for a number of years.

The Cross on the Hill. *John Myers.*

Metal artwork depicting the resurrection of Christ, created by prisoners at Fort Leavenworth, Kansas. *John Myers.*

Engaging with Bill, one quickly realizes he is a man of faith. He spoke about the fifteen individuals from DuBois, St. Marys and Weedville who recognized in 1987 that there was something distinctive about the location where the cross is now standing. He described the group as a small interfaith prayer group—a nondenominational group, if you will. They began to experience signs and wonders at that location. The group reached out to pastors and priests regarding their experiences, and they prayed often. Eventually, the group took the name the Holy Family and were able to lease an acre of land to place a cross. At the dedication in August 1990, almost as a sign of recognition of the specialness of this place, the elk bugled for an hour while the members and clergy prayed.

The Holy Family group has since acquired the title to the land. Assisted by an attorney, the Holy Family as a group has been structured to pass the property along; it does not belong to individuals. Registered as Holy Family, a charitable organization, its main purpose is religion-related spiritual development.

In 2014, a walkway to the cross was constructed by Eagle Scout Christopher Lang and Girl Scout Katherine Lang leading from the parking lot to the cross. The signs with Bible verses were added to assist those who may have difficulty walking to the cross to experience the specialness of the location.

The first baptism at the Cross on the Hill was held on Sunday, August 21, 2022. Family and friends gathered as a nine-month-old girl from DuBois was baptized by the pastor of the Austin United Methodist Church. "The cross has been the site of many proposals, weddings, vow renewals, interfaith healing services, Sunday school classes and personal meditation sessions."[371]

For those who haven't experienced the Cross on the Hill, a YouTube video titled "The Cross on the Hill Interfaith Memorial, 2016," created by Darrin Gennocro, shows breathtaking views of the cross and the area around it, from both the ground and the air.

MT. ZION CEMETERY AND MT. ZION HISTORIC PARK

Continuing on Mt. Zion Road past the Cross on the Hill leads one to the location of Mt. Zion Cemetery, which was adjacent to the oldest Protestant church in Elk County, Mt. Zion Church, which burned to the ground on September 1, 1976. The oldest part of the cemetery contains the remains of early settlers in the region, including Peter Pearsall and his wife, who set

Mt. Zion Church. *Ancestry.com, Boston1635 family tree.*

aside land for the cemetery and church, and early settler Erasmus Morey, portrayed in an earlier chapter. The cemetery is in active use today.

Just past the cemetery lies Mt. Zion Historic Park, an amazing undertaking by locals to not only commemorate the location of the church but also display the history of the region.

Peter Pearsall, who donated the land for the church and cemetery, was one of those who came into the region because of the vast timber reserves available. Born in 1769 in Dutchess County, New York, Peter served in the War of 1812 and was awarded bounty lands by the U.S. government for his service in the war. He learned the trades of millwright and iron worker from his father, and he became an expert in forging tools and equipment for use in the timber industry. By 1793, he had a farm and sawmill in Saratoga County, New York.[372]

Unfortunately, Pearsall had some financial misfortunes and lost his farm and sawmill. Traveling to New York City in 1817, he was put in touch with an agent for the Holland Land Company, mentioned in an earlier chapter. The company was advertising the availability of land in Pennsylvania, hoping to move along some of the land in this region, and it was looking for someone with experience in sawmills and harvesting timber to work on its behalf. Pearsall was the perfect candidate.

The Holland Land Company persuaded Pearsall to come to this area and inspect the land. In the rugged terrain that lay before him, Pearsall saw vast forests of hemlock, oak, hickory, white pine and chestnut and realized the potential for money to be made in the timber industry in this region.[373]

Receiving the backing he needed from the Holland Land Company, he purchased large tracts of white pine. In the spring of 1824, he moved to Sinnemahoning with his new wife, Hannah, before moving up the Bennett's Branch to a farm near what is now Caledonia.[374]

Realizing the need for a place to hold religious services, Pearsall opened his home for services. But he had a larger vision: to construct a Protestant church. In 1832, Pearsall donated land from his farm for a church and cemetery. Unfortunately, Peter Pearsall died in 1838, before the church was built. He was the first person to be buried at Mt. Zion Cemetery.[375]

The task of building the church fell to his son, Alfred Pearsall. Construction of the church began in 1850. It was finished in 1856, at a cost of $2,000. The church was dedicated as a Baptist church, but in accordance with Peter Pearsall's wish, it was open to all Protestant faiths. Through the years, it was supported by donations, box socials and name quilts donated by the people of the area who were interested in the welfare of the church.[376]

The church was used actively until 1913, when it had no pastor. From that time until 1926, the church was neglected. Once again, the good citizens of the area stepped in, raising money for repairs and upkeep. For a number of years, sunrise services were held at Easter and on Mt. Zion Homecoming Day, the first Sunday in September. Sadly, the use of the building came to an end on September 1, 1976. A fire of suspicious origin broke out, burning the building to the ground. The annual Homecoming Day had already been scheduled for September 5, and despite the loss of the beloved building, the Mt. Zion Day Committee erected a large tent at the site of the razed church and carried out its annual Homecoming Day services.[377]

It was the vision of local resident and businessman Joe Burke that led to the formation of the Mt. Zion Historical Society and to the building of the Mt. Zion Historic Park, headed up by Burke's son, Jim.[378]

A large parking area is adjacent to Mt. Zion Road and the park. Passing under a sign that reads, "Welcome, Mt. Zion Historic Park," one's eye is quickly drawn to a walkway of memorial stones listing the United States' wars and memorial stones with the names of veterans from the region who served their country. Off to the side, a highly polished bench has been placed "In Memory of Vietnam Veterans," and a reference to those veterans of the Bucktail Chapter, 720 of the Vietnam War.

A beautiful memorial lists the history of the Mt. Zion Church and Alfred Pearsall, who undertook its construction. Another monument bears the inscription, "The people of Bennetts Valley dedicate this memorial to all American veterans both living and deceased," with a plaque dedicated to

Mt. Zion Historic Park sign. *John Myers.*

Vietnam veterans' memorial bench at Mt. Zion Historic Park. *John Myers.*

Memorial to Alfred Pearsall and Mt. Zion Church history, Mt. Zion Historic Park. *John Myers.*

Freedom Bell, Mt. Zion Historic Park. *John Myers.*

Frederick Weed, founder of Weedville and Revolutionary War soldier, on the right side of the stone and to Isaac Webb, another Revolutionary War soldier and founder of nearby Force, on the left side of the stone.

An impressive Freedom Bell carries an inscription, "This bell represents all the bells that tolled during and after America's Wars. May Americans forever remember the price of freedom, and those who have sacrificed to pay the price." Nearby is a memorial to the Civil War with a likeness of Thomas Winslow of Benezette, who was the highest-ranking native of Elk County to serve in the Bucktail Regiment.

At one point, a pile of stones is identified as the original foundation stones of the Mt. Zion Church; a plaque notes the effort it took to place them on the property prior to building the church.

Markers highlighting the United States' wars and the veterans from the region who served in them are a reminder of the quote, "Freedom isn't free." The Mt. Zion Historic Park is well worth a visit.

CONCLUSION

Rebecca Harding Davis (1831–1910), American author and Pennsylvania native, captured the essence of the Wilds when she wrote,
"Nowhere else in this country, from sea to sea, does nature comfort us with such assurance of plenty, such rich and tranquil beauty as in those unsung, unpainted hills of Pennsylvania."[379]

There is something specific about the words "those unsung, unpainted hills of Pennsylvania" that applies to travel along the Benezette corridor when passing through the villages named in this book. The hills—or, as some call them, mountains—are so steep and high that they give one the feeling of being wrapped in the lush forest vegetation that grows there: a feeling of peace and safety.

The forests, which provide wild vegetation and a variety of trees, such as oak, cherry, maple, beech, birch, poplar, hemlock and white pine among others, provide food and safety for animals and birds that make their home in this region of the Wilds.

We have followed its early history from Native Americans to early settlers to those who brought industry into the region. As you reflect on the vast forests growing today, imagine the experiences of those settlers when they came into this "howling wilderness."

Native forest fruit was then abundant, game was plenty, the rivers were streams of crystal liquid. Women frequently performed a part of the farm service in that age, some with sickle and rake in hand doing the work of a harvest man. Others with hoe and fork did good work in the hay and corn field. One of them is remembered as placing her child in a sap-trough near-by, when but little over a week old, while she split more rails in a day than her husband.[380]

Men travelled miles on foot or by river to get much-needed supplies for their families. They developed many skills, including blacksmithing and gunsmithing, and they built cabins for their first homes. The women, brought into the wilderness, were isolated from the outside world, raising their children without doctors and nurses, making candles for use in the home, cooking and baking with basic items, growing and preserving foods from their gardens and salting and preserving game brought in by the men. Women washed clothes in a tub with a washboard outdoors in water carried from wells or streams.

In later history, the trees were stripped from the land and sent downriver to the large lumber markets in Pennsylvania and Maryland, and the hills were left empty and barren. The coal and gas industries also left marks on the landscape.

Today, with a shift toward tourism, people are coming to catch a glimpse of the elk reintroduced in 1913, as well as other wildlife that have multiplied under the direction of the Pennsylvania Game Commission. The Pennsylvania Department of Conservation and Natural Resources, responsible for maintaining and preserving the state's 124 state parks and twenty state forests, has played an important role by engaging in conservation practices that allow visitors to the region to experience the out-of-doors.[381]

When visitors arrive, they are greeted by locals, many of whose families have been here since the early 1800s, while others are the descendants of later immigrants who passed through Castle Garden and Ellis Island, both in New York State, on their way to the Wilds.

I myself have many fond memories of the Benezette area, which I visited on a regular basis with my parents and grandmother, and our relatives on Winslow Hill. I remember the gas boom, when a family from Oklahoma, Mr. and Mrs. Oswald and their two children, rented my uncle's cabin to live, work and go to school in the region during those years. I recall walking from Winslow Hill down a dirt (and dusty) road into Benezette to buy stick candy at the old Benezette Store on Front Street and a humorous story about my uncle loading me and the Glaxner boy from the farm down the road into the back of his old Ford pickup truck, driving down Winslow Hill Road past the

Methodist church where his wife, my aunt, was attending a meeting of the Woman's Christian Temperance Union (WCTU) and pulling alongside the Benezette Hotel, where he ducked in for a quick drink. Our lips were sealed by the bribe he brought from the hotel: individual bags of potato chips.

Working on this book and reaching out to people with questions during my research, I felt a kinship with them. While some of them are, in fact, my kin a few generations removed, others willingly provided answers to my questions, another sort of kinship between those of us who have been reared in the Pennsylvania Wilds.

This book was written to provide those unfamiliar with the region a glimpse of its history, which led to the experiences that await today's visitors. It may also provide frequent visitors and locals with some new information about the Benezette corridor, also referred to as the Benezette Wilds.

As my family history goes back to 1806 in the Benezette Wilds, I appreciate the uniqueness of the region. "Lose (or find!) yourself in the Pennsylvania Wilds lifestyle: A slower pace where the way of life is intertwined with nature and stewardship."[382]

NOTES

Preface

1. Pennsylvania Wilds, "About the Pennsylvania Wilds."

Introduction

2. Pennsylvania Great Outdoors Visitors Bureau, "Discover Benezette."
3. Keystone Elk Country Alliance, "Elk Country Visitor Center."
4. Pennsylvania Great Outdoors Visitors Bureau, "Mt. Zion Historical Park";
   Pennsylvania Wilds, "Quehanna Wild Area."
5. Wessman, *History of Elk County*, 289.

Chapter 1

6. National Park Service, "Treaty of Stanwix."
7. McKnight, *Pioneer Outline History*, 498.
8. Wallace, *Indians in Pennsylvania*, 165.
9. Donehoo, *History*, 206
10. Burke, "Indian Mill."
11. J.H. Beers & Co., *McKean, Elk, Cameron and Potter, Pennsylvania*, 819–20.
12. Meginness, *Journal of Samuel Maclay*, 61, 62.
13. Ibid., 22.
14. Jones, *Juniata Valley*, 253.
15. Founders Online, "To George Washington."
16. Meginness, *Journal of Samuel Maclay*, 23.
17. Ibid., 29.

18. Ibid., 25.
19. Ibid., 25, 26.
20. J.H. Beers & Co., *McKean, Elk, Cameron and Potter, Pennsylvania*, 825.
21. Penn Libraries, University of Pennsylvania, "James Potter, 1729–1789."
22. Ibid.
23. Ibid.
24. J.H. Beers & Co., *McKean, Elk and Forest, Pennsylvania*, 584.
25. Holton and Holton, *Winslow Memorial*, 993.
26. Pennsylvania Great Outdoors Visitors Bureau, "Big Elk Lick."

Chapter 2

27. Wessman, *History of Elk County*, 280.
28. *Lancaster (PA) Intelligencer*, February 28, 1809.
29. Holton and Holton, *Winslow Memorial*, 998.
30. Ibid.
31. *United States Gazette*, September 24, 1817.
32. "Winslow Family Reunion," *Ridgway Record*.
33. "Benezette," *Elk County Advocate*.
34. Ibid.
35. Punxsutawney Area Historical & Genealogical Society, *Following the Drinking Gourd*.
36. "Minish Home Slave Pit," *Punxsutawney Spirit*.
37. Wessman, *History of Elk County*, 280.
38. Ibid., 17.
39. Aldrich, *History of Clearfield County*, 324.
40. Holton and Holton, *Winslow Memorial*, 998.
41. Wessman, *History of Elk County*, 288, 289.
42. Ibid., 289.
43. Ibid.
44. U.S. Census Bureau, "Benezette Township, PA."
45. J.H. Beers & Co., *McKean, Elk and Forest, Pennsylvania*, 589.
46. Scotthoskins, "U.S. History 1800–1817 Timeline."
47. History.com Editors, "George Washington."
48. Britannica, "Era of Good Feelings."
49. Meginness, *Journal of Samuel Maclay*, 23.
50. Wessman, *History of Elk County*, 260.
51. Meginness, *Journal of Samuel Maclay*, 23.
52. Wessman, *History of Elk County*, 280.
53. Egle, *Commonwealth of Pennsylvania*, 685.
54. J.H. Beers & Co., *McKean, Elk and Forest, Pennsylvania*, 585.
55. "Laying the Cornerstone," *Elk County Advocate*; "Morey," *Valley Echo*.
56. "Laying the Cornerstone."
57. Ibid.
58. Wessman, *History of Elk County*, 299, 300.
59. Ibid.

60. "Erasmus Morey," *Pittsburgh Dispatch*.
61. "Morey."
62. J.H. Beers & Co., *McKean, Elk and Forest, Pennsylvania*, 779.
63. Ibid.
64. "Lonesome Grave on Rock Hill," *Courier-Express*.
65. Ibid.
66. "About Early Settlers," *Gettysburg Times*.
67. Ibid.

Chapter 3

68. "Weedville," *Elk County Advocate*.
69. Wessman, *History of Elk County*, 382.
70. Ibid.
71. Crocco, *Brief History*.
72. MacLean, "Caledonia."
73. Britannica, "Caledonia."
74. Wessman, *History of Elk County*, 382; House of Names, "Warner History."
75. Olson, "Kincaid Family Tree."
76. J.H. Beers & Co., *McKean, Elk, Cameron and Potter, Pennsylvania*, 597.
77. Wessman, *History of Elk County*, 382.
78. Ibid.
79. "Defying the Law," *Elk County Advocate*.
80. Ibid.
81. Ibid.
82. "Trial Opened," *Elk County Advocate*.
83. "Insurance Settlement," *Kane Republican*.
84. "Shoemaker Cuts the Throat," *Cambria Freeman*.
85. "Love and Jealousy," *Valley Sentinel*.
86. Ibid.
87. Ibid.
88. Wessman, *History of Elk County*, 292.
89. Ibid., 284.
90. Ibid., 292.
91. "Early Air Mail Days," *Courier-Express*.
92. Ibid.
93. Pennsylvania Great Outdoors Visitors Bureau, "Medix Hotel."
94. Ibid.
95. Ibid.
96. Wessman, *History of Elk County*, 291.
97. Pennsylvania State Grange, "Pennsylvania Granges."
98. Ibid.
99. "Galaxy Album."
100. Buffalo Architecture and History, "John D. Larkin."
101. Tokugawa Antiques, "Larkin Soap Company Premiums."
102. Wessman, *History of Elk County*, 284.

103. "Our Schools," *Elk County Advocate*.
104. Winslow House Heritage Council, *History Lessons*.
105. Ibid.
106. Wessman, *History of Elk County*, 283.
107. "Yesterday's Dark Spell," *Kane Republican*.
108. Wessman, *History of Elk County*, 285.
109. "Darkness on the Edge," *Daily Press*.
110. "Yesterday's Dark Spell."
111. Field, "1950 Great Smoke Pall."
112. Ibid.
113. West, "Elk County: Stations."
114. Ibid.
115. J.H. Beers & Co., *McKean, Elk, Cameron and Potter, Pennsylvania*, 778.
116. Ibid., 289.
117. Taylor, "Presidential Legends."
118. "Centennial Scrapbook," *Kane Republican*.
119. "Presidential Legends."
120. "Dear Advocate," *Elk County Advocate*.
121. Ibid.
122. Wessman, *History of Elk County*, 291.
123. Ibid.
124. Ibid., 99.
125. Ibid.
126. Ibid.
127. Ibid.
128. Ibid., 100.
129. Ibid.
130. Weidenboerner, "Historian Shocked."
131. "Hunters Sue," Associated Press.
132. "FBI to Hand Over," Associated Press.
133. Rubinkam, "Witnesses to FBI Hunt."
134. Ibid.
135. Ibid.
136. Ibid.
137. Ibid.
138. Pennsylvania Game Commission, "Elk Viewing Destinations."
139. J.H. Beers & Co., *McKean, Elk, Cameron and Potter, Pennsylvania*, 825.
140. Meginness, *Journal of Samuel Maclay*, 22.
141. Wessman, *History of Elk County*, 297–98.
142. Ibid., 298.
143. Ibid.
144. Ibid.
145. Ibid., 299.
146. J.H. Beers & Co., *McKean, Elk, Cameron and Potter, Pennsylvania*, 584.
147. Rootsweb, "John Barr."
148. Ancestry.com, "U.S. Army Register."

149. ExplorePAHistory, "Tom Mix Historic Marker."
150. Heimel, "Tom Mix Memory Fades."
151. Ibid.
152. Powell, "Castle Garden."
153. Library of Congress, "Castle Garden Bridge," 10.
154. Ibid.
155. "Dig Day at Driftwood," *Cameron County Press*.
156. J.H. Beers & Co., *McKean, Elk, Cameron and Potter, Pennsylvania*, 825.
157. U.S. Census Bureau, "Driftwood, PA."
158. Library of Congress, "Castle Garden Bridge," 10.
159. "Driftwood," *Cameron County Press-Emporium Independent*.
160. Ibid.
161. Ibid.
162. "Do You Remember?" *Cameron County Press*.
163. Pennsylvania Great Outdoors Visitors Bureau, "Bucktail Overlook."
164. Donehoo, *Indian Villages*, 206.
165. *Valley Girl Views*, "Great Runaway of 1778."
166. J.H. Beers & Co., *McKean, Elk, Cameron and Potter, Pennsylvania*, 823.
167. Ibid., 824.
168. Bennett, "Village of Sinnemahoning."
169. Independent Order of Odd Fellows, https://odd-fellows.org.
170. Collins, *Royally Rugged Cameron County*, 4.
171. "Sinnemahoning Liars Club," *Cameron County Press*.
172. PA Department of Conservation and Natural Resources, "Sinnemahoning State Park."
173. Pennsylvania Great Outdoors Visitors Bureau, "George B. Stevenson Reservoir."

Chapter 4

174. Wallace, *Indians in Pennsylvania*, 84.
175. Ibid., 172.
176. Ibid., 166.
177. Wallace, *Conrad Weiser*, 21.
178. Wallace, *Indians in Pennsylvania*, 63.
179. Ibid., 64, 68, 69.
180. Ibid., 166.
181. Ibid., 168.
182. Ibid., 75.
183. Wessman, *History of Elk County*, 44.
184. McKnight, *Pioneer Outline History*, 276.
185. "Oldest Settler," *Renovo Record*.
186. Ibid.
187. Collins, *Royally Rugged Cameron County*, 2.
188. *Cameron County PA News*, "1860 Journal."
189. "Cameron County Historical Society, *Journal of Thomas Hollen*, 45.
190. Ibid., 41.

191. Cameron County Genealogy Project, Grove Township, "Methodist Episcopal Church."
192. Collins, *Royally Rugged Cameron County*, 4.
193. "Penfield, PA, Aug. 7, 1876, Editor Advocate," *Elk County Advocate* (Ridgway, PA), August 10, 1876.
194. J.H. Beers & Co., *McKean, Elk and Forest, Pennsylvania*, 586.
195. Collins, *Royally Rugged Cameron County*, 4.
196. J.H. Beers & Co., *McKean, Elk, Cameron and Potter, Pennsylvania*, 953.
197. Ibid., 3, 4.

Chapter 5

198. Edwards and Cobb, "School Days, School Days."
199. Wessman, *History of Elk County*, 284.
200. "Our Schools," *Elk County Advocate*.
201. Ibid.
202. Ibid.
203. Ibid.
204. Ibid.
205. Ibid.
206. "Educational Notes," *Elk County Advocate*.
207. Huntley, *Sinnamahone*, 41–42.
208. Wessman, *History of Elk County*, 284.
209. Ibid.
210. Ibid., 285.
211. "Benezette Township Receives $10,000," *St. Marys Daily Press*.
212. "SMASD Gifts," *Courier-Express*.

Chapter 6

213. Gavlock, "Forgotten Heritage."
214. Pennsylvania Lumber Museum, "Lumber Heritage."
215. Kane Area Development Center, "History of Kane."
216. J.H. Beers & Co., *McKean, Elk, Cameron and Potter, Pennsylvania*, 825.
217. Cox, "Transition in the Woods," 345, 346.
218. Ibid., 346.
219. Ibid., 347.
220. Rogers, *Rafting Days*.
221. Huntley, *Sinnemahone*, 8.
222. Ibid., 14.
223. Wessman, *History of Elk County*, 382.
224. Gavlock, "Forgotten Heritage."
225. Huntley, *Sinnemahone*, 186.
226. Ibid.
227. Ibid., 187.

228. Ibid., 188.
229. Ibid., 188, 189.
230. Cox, "Transition in the Woods," 348.
231. Ibid., 350.
232. Aldrich, *History of Clearfield County*, 719.
233. Ibid.
234. Ibid., 720.
235. Ibid.
236. ExplorePAHistory, "Susquehanna Log Boom."
237. Cox, "Transition in the Woods," 351.
238. Ibid., 352, 353.
239. Aldrich, *History of Clearfield County*, 559, 560.
240. Ibid., 360.
241. Ibid.
242. Cox, "Transition in the Woods," 352.
243. Ibid., 363.
244. J.H. Beers & Co., *McKean, Elk and Forest, Pennsylvania*, 625, 626.
245. Ibid., 626.
246. Ibid.
247. "Railroad," *Brookville Republican*.
248. Ibid.
249. Ibid.
250. "Timber—Coal," *Courier-Express*.
251. "Railroads."
252. Nay, "Winslow Colliery Railroad."
253. "More Railroad," *Clearfield Republican*.
254. Levine and Nay, "Bennetts Valley, Railroads."
255. Burns, "Doodlebug Rail Cars."
256. J.H. Beers & Co., *McKean, Elk and Forest, Pennsylvania*, 631.
257. Ibid.
258. Wessman, *History of Elk County*, 281–82.
259. Ibid., 282.
260. Ibid.
261. Ibid.
262. Ibid., 385.
263. Ibid., 384.
264. Ibid.
265. Ibid.
266. Ibid., 383.
267. J.H. Beers & Co., *McKean, Elk, Cameron and Potter, Pennsylvania*, 673–74.
268. Mt. Zion Historical Society, "Cooking of Coal."
269. Ibid.
270. "Man, Made Rich," *Progress*.
271. J.H. Beers & Co., *McKean, Elk and Forest, Pennsylvania*, 574, 577.
272. U.S. Energy Information Administration, "Pennsylvania State Energy Profile."
273. Historical Marker Database, "Leidy Natural Gas Boom."

274. Wessman, *History of Elk County*, 287, 288.
275. "Bennetts Valley Gas Boom," *Kane Republican*.
276. Wessman, *History of Elk County*, 288.
277. "Day by Day Chronology," *Progress*.
278. "State Sees Benezette Area," *Progress*.
279. "Landowners of Medix Run," *Progress*.
280. Ibid.
281. Wessman, *History of Elk County*, 288.

Chapter 7

282. "Bucktails," *Cameron County Press*.
283. "Monument to the Bucktails," *Cameron County Press*.
284. Grow, "Thomas L. Kane," 5, 11.
285. "Robert Gray Taylor," *Kane Republican*.
286. Grow, "Thomas L. Kane," 12
287. "War Begun," *Clearfield Republican*.
288. Pennsylvania Historic and Museum Commission, "Forty-Second Regiment."
289. Wessman, *History of Elk County*, 50.
290. Howard, *History of the Bucktails*, 11, 12, 13.
291. Ibid.
292. Ibid., 14.
293. Pennsylvania Historic and Museum Commission, "Guide for Classroom Teachers"; Pennsylvania Historic and Museum Commission, "Forty-Second Regiment."
294. "Why Was It," *Elk Horn*.

Chapter 8

295. History.com Editors, "Civilian Conservation Corps."
296. PA Department of Conservation and Natural Resources, "Hicks Run."
297. PA Department of Conservation and Natural Resources, "Civilian Conservation Corps."
298. Ibid.
299. Ibid.
300. Pennsylvania Wilds, "Quehanna Wild Area."
301. National Archives, "Atoms for Peace."
302. Curtiss-Wright Corporation, "Over 90 Years."
303. ExplorePAHistory, "Joseph T. Rothrock Historical Marker."
304. Ibid.
305. Ibid.
306. Liquisearch, "State Forests."
307. Wessman, *History of Elk County*, 282
308. Liquisearch, "Atoms for Peace."
309. Merriam-Webster, "Freshet"; Donehoo, *Indian Villages*, 215.

310. Wallace, *Indians in Pennsylvania*, 12.
311. Wessman, *History of Elk County*, 282.
312. "Curtiss-Wright, Penn State," *Progress*.
313. Pennsylvania Wilds, "Quehanna Wild Area."
314. Liquisearch, "Atoms for Peace."
315. Liquisearch, "Quehanna Wild Area."
316. Smrekar, "Memories."
317. Pennsylvania Conservation Heritage Project, "Marion E. Brooks."
318. "Monument, Forest Tract," *Progress*.
319. "Memories," *Courier-Express*.
320. Ibid.
321. Ibid.
322. "Monument, Forest Tract."
323. Ibid.
324. ExplorePAHistory, "Beaver Run Dam."
325. Glessner, "5 Best Roadside Attractions."
326. Ibid.
327. PA Department of Conservation and Natural Resources, "Teaberry Loop Trail."
328. Glessner, "5 Best Roadside Attractions."
329. Ibid.
330. Pennsylvania Great Outdoors Visitors Bureau, "Great Motorcycle Rides."

Chapter 9

331. "Elk, PA's Largest," *Philadelphia Inquirer*.
332. Ibid.
333. Ibid.
334. Mulvihill, "Tribute to 'Freddy.'"
335. Ibid.
336. Fagan, "Elk or Wapiti."
337. Hill, "Fred Jr."
338. Ibid.
339. Pennsylvania Game Commission, "Wildlife Notes."
340. Ibid.
341. Ibid.
342. Hill, "Fred Jr."
343. Mulvihill, "Tribute to 'Freddy.'"
344. "Story of Fred, Gentle Giant," *Williamsport Sun-Gazette*.
345. Ibid.
346. Ibid.
347. Mulvihill, "Tribute to 'Freddy.'"
348. Ibid.
349. Ibid.
350. Kosack, "History of Pennsylvania Elk."
351. Meginness, *Journal of Samuel Maclay*, 30.
352. Kosack, "History of Pennsylvania Elk."

353. Ibid.
354. "Elk Are Dying," *Harrisburg Daily Independent*.
355. Kosack, "History of Pennsylvania Elk."
356. "Elk Management Area Proposed," *Progress*.
357. Elk Country Visitor Center, "(Re)Introducing the Elk."
358. "Elk, PA's Largest," *Philadelphia Inquirer*.
359. Banfield and Rosenberry, *Elk Management in Pennsylvania*.
360. Ibid.
361. Ibid.
362. Ibid.
363. Graffius, "Pennsylvania Game Commission Rescues."
364. Ibid.

Chapter 10

365. *New Webster's Dictionary and Thesaurus*.
366. Ibid.
367. Graffius, "Chapel Built in Benezette."
368. *PA Elk Country* (blog), "Directions to the Cross."
369. Glessner, "Visiting the Cross."
370. Ibid.
371. Brooks, "First Baptism."
372. Pearsall, "History and Genealogy," 1,130.
373. Ibid.
374. Ibid.
375. Jesberger, "Pioneer Spirit."
376. Wessman, *History of Elk County*, 44.
377. Ibid., 45.
378. Jesberger, "Pioneer Spirit."

Conclusion

379. Pennsylvania Wilds, "About the Pennsylvania Wilds."
380. J.H. Beers & Co., *McKean, Elk and Forest, Pennsylvania*, 589.
381. PA Department of Conservation and Natural Resources, "About DCNR."
382. Pennsylvania Wilds, "About the Pennsylvania Wilds."

BIBLIOGRAPHY

Aldrich, Lewis Cass. *History of Clearfield County, PA*. Syracuse, NY: D. Mason, 1887.

Ancestry.com. "U.S. Army Register of Enlistments, 1798–1914." https://www. ancestry.com.

Associated Press. "Hunters Sue for Records on FBI's Civil War Gold Dig in Elk County." January 5, 2022.

———. "Judge: FBI to Hand Over Elk County Civil War Gold Hunt Records." April 19, 2022. https://www.wtaj.com/news/local-news/judge-fbi-to-hand-over-elk-county-civil-war-gold-hunt-records/.

Bainfield, Jeremy, and Christopher Rosenberry. *Elk Management in Pennsylvania, A Five-Year Plan (2020–2025)*. Pennsylvania Game Commission. https://www.pgc. pa/gov/Wildlife/WildlifeSpecies/Elk/Document/Elk%20Management%20 Plan%202020-2025.pdf.

Bennett, Pete. "The Village of Sinnemahoning, PA." *Highland Gazette*, May 1996. Found at Cameron County Genealogy Project. https://www.pa-roots.com/ cameron/.

Britannica. "Caledonia." www.britannica.com/place/Caledonia.

———. "Era of Good Feelings." www.britannica.com/event/Era-of-Good-Feelings.

Brooks, Kathy. "First Baptism at the Cross on the Hill." *Potter Leader-Enterprise*, August 22, 2022. https://www.tiogapublishing.com/potter_leader_enterprise/ community/first-baptism-at-the-cross-on-the-hill/article_9ad75e1a-222c-11ed-a650-a385c517d4b8.html.

Brookville (PA) Republican. "Railroad." December 5, 1866.

———. "Railroads." April 22, 1868.

Buffalo Architecture and History. "John D. Larkin—Biography." https://www. buffaloah.com/h/larkin/index.html.

Burke, Jim. "The Indian Mill at Medix Run." Mt. Zion Historical Society. https:// mtzionhistoricalsociety.org/history/stories/the-indian-mill-at-medix-run/.

Burns, Adam. "Doodlebug Rail Cars." American-Rails.com, last revised June 22, 2023. https://www.american-rails.com/doodlebugs.html.

Cambria Freeman (Ebensburg, PA). "A Shoemaker Cuts the Throat of Another Man's Wife, Confesses the Deed and Then Cuts His Own Throat." June 30, 1876.

Cameron County Genealogy Project, Grove Township. "Methodist Episcopal Church—Sinnemahoning Circuit 1867–1894." https://sites.rootsweb.com/~pacamero/township/grove/methodist.html.

Cameron County Historical Society. *The 1860 Journal of Thomas Hollen, Circuit Riding Minister.* Emporium, PA: Cameron County Historical Society, May 2023.

Cameron County PA News (blog). "Cameron County Historical Society Releases 'The 1860 Journal of Thomas Hollen Circuit Riding Minister.'" May 26, 2023. https://cameroncountynews.blogspot.com/2023/05/cc-historical-society-releases-1860.html.

Cameron County Press (Emporium, PA). "The Bucktails." April 30, 1908.

———. "Dig Day at Driftwood." April 30, 1908.

———. "Do You Remember?" April 21, 1960.

———. "Monument to the Bucktails." May 9, 1907.

———. "Sinnemahoning Liars Club." September 28, 1899.

Cameron County Press-Emporium Independent (Emporium, PA). "Driftwood—Once a Bustling Town." February 18, 1960.

Clearfield Republican (Clearfield, PA). "More Railroad." March 31, 1869.

———. "The War Begun." April 17, 1861.

Collins, Ira. *Royally Rugged Cameron County.* Sykesville, PA: Nupp, 1976.

Courier-Express (DuBois, PA). "Early Air Mail Days in This Area 50 Years Ago." December 29, 1977.

———. "The Saga of the Lonesome Grave on Rock Hill." March 29, 1974.

———. "SMASD Gifts Bennetts Valley Elementary School Building to Jay Township." June 13, 2023.

———. "Timber—Coal Spurred Arrival of Railroads." July 2, 1976.

Cox, Thomas R. "Transition in the Woods: Log Drivers, Raftsmen and the Emergence of Modern Lumbering in Pennsylvania." *Magazine of History and Biography* 104, no. 3 (July 1980): 345–64. https://www.jstor.org/stable/20091486.

Crocco, S.R. *Brief History of Bennetts Valley and St. Joseph Church.* 1972. https://liturgicalcenter.org/media/parish_pdf/E/e-12.1.pdf.

Curtiss-Wright Corporation. "Over 90 Years of Growth." https://www.curtisswright.com/company/history.

Daily Press (St. Marys, PA). "Benezette Township Receives $10,000 for 'Old Benezette Schoolhouse.'" July 6, 2023.

———. "Darkness on the Edge of Town." September 19, 1990.

Donehoo, Dr. George P. *A History of the Indian Villages and Place Names in Pennsylvania.* Lewisburg, PA: Wennawoods Publishing, 2010.

Edwards, Gus (music), and Will D. Cobb (lyrics). "School Days, School Days." New York: Gus Edwards Music Publishing, 1907.

Egle, William H. *An Illustrated History of the Commonwealth of Pennsylvania.* Harrisburg, PA: Dewitt C. Goodrich, 1876.

Elk County Advocate (Ridgway, PA). "Benezette." January 13, 1881.

———. "Dear Advocate." June 12, 1873.

———. "Defying the Law." April 22, 1880.

———. "Educational Notes." June 16, 1881.

———. "Laying the Cornerstone." July 24, 1879.

———. "Our Schools." January 27, 1881.

———. "Penfield, PA, August 7, 1876." August 10, 1876.

———. "The Trial Opened." September 30, 1880.

———. "Weedville, July 11, 1874." July 16, 1874.

Elk Country Visitor Center. "History: (Re)Introducing the Elk." https://elkcountryvisitorcenter.com/learn-overview/history/.

ExplorePAHistory. "Beaver Run Dam Wildlife Viewing Area Attraction Details." https://explorepahistory.com/attraction.php?id=1-B-2ADD.

———. "Joseph T. Rothrock Historical Marker." https://explorepahistory.com/hmarker.php?markerId=1-A-146.

———. "The Susquehanna Log Boom, Williamsport, 1890." https://explorepahistory.com/~expa/displayimage.php?imgId=1-2-34C.

———. "Tom Mix Historic Marker." https://explorepahistory.com/hmarker.php?markerId=1-A-263.

Fagan, Damian. "Elk or Wapiti, *Cervus elaphas*—Elk, Deer, and Moose Family—Cervidae." DesertUSA. https://www.desertusa.com/animals/elk.html.

Field, Robert. "Revisiting the 1950 Great Smoke Pall." *Canadian Smoke Newsletter* (Fall 2008): 13–15. https://www-air.larc.nasa.gov/missions/arctas/docs/CanadianSmokeNwsltr_Feb2009.pdf.

Founders Online. "To George Washington from William Patterson, 3 April, 1779." https://founders.archives.gov/documents/Washington/03-19-02-0682.

"Galaxy Album." Yiddish to English translation by Ruth Ratson. Philadelphia, Pennsylvania, 2019.

Gavlock, Erin L. "Forgotten Heritage." Pennsylvania Center for the Book, Summer 2009. https://pabook.libraries.psu.edu/literary-cultural-heritage-map-pa/feature-articles/forgotten-heritage.

Gettysburg (PA) Times. "A Bit of History about Early Settlers." October 11, 1963.

Glessner, Rusty. "The 5 Best Roadside Attractions in the Quehanna Wild Area." Pennsylvania Bucket List. https://pabucketlist.com/the-5-best-roadside-attractions-in-the-quehanna-wild-area.

———. "Visiting the Cross on the Hill in Elk County." https://pabucketlist.com/visiting-the-cross-on-the-hill-in-elk-county.

Graffius, Ryan. "Pennsylvania Game Commission Rescues Elk Trapped in Telephone Wire in Cameron County." WJAC, September 29, 2023. https://wjactv.com/news/local/gallery-game-commission-pennsylvania-elk-animals-rescue-trapped-telephone-wire-cameron-sinnemahoning-wildlife.

Grow, Matthew J. "Thomas L. Kane and Nineteenth-Century American Culture." *BYU Studies Quarterly* 48, no. 4 (2009): 13–24. https://scholarsarchive.byu.edu/byusq/vol48/iss4/3.

Harrisburg (PA) Daily Independent. "Elk Are Dying." April 21, 1913.

Heimel, Paul. "Tom Mix Memory Fades in Cameron County." *Bradford (PA) Era*, September 13, 2007.

Hill, Willard C. "Fred Jr. 'Bull No. 36' Pennsylvania's Most Famous Elk." *Pennsylvania Wildlife Photographer* (blog), September 16, 2010. http://pawildlifephotographer.blogspot.com/2010/09/fred-jr-bull-no-36-pennsylvanias-most.html.

Historical Marker Database. "Leidy Natural Gas Boom." https://www.hmdb.org/m.asp?m=65551.

History.com Editors. "Civilian Conservation Corps." www.history.com/topics/great-depression.

———. "George Washington, Facts, Revolution and Presidency." https://www.history.com/topics/us-presidents/george-washington.

Holton, David Parsons, and Frances K. Holton. *Winslow Memorial, 1888.* Vol. 2. New York: D.P. Holton, 1888.

House of Names. "Warner History, Family Crest & Coats of Arms." https://www.houseofnames.com/warner-family-crest.

Howard, Thomas O.R. *History of the Bucktails—Kane Rifle Regiment of Pennsylvania Reserve Corp., 13th Pennsylvania Reserves, 42 of the Line.* Philadelphia: Philadelphia Electric, 1873.

Huntley, George William. *Sinnemahone: A Story of Great Trees and Powerful Men.* Boston: Christopher, 1945.

Independent Order of Odd Fellows. https://odd-fellows.org.

Jesberger, Sherry. "Pioneer Spirit: The Pearsall Family and Mt. Zion Church." Mt. Zion Historical Society, 2002. https://mtzionhistoricalsociety.org/history/mt-zion-church/pioneer-spirit-the-pearsall-family-and-mt-zion-church/.

J.H. Beers & Company. *History of the Counties of McKean, Elk and Forest, Pennsylvania* […]. Chicago: 1890.

———. *History of the Counties of McKean, Elk, Cameron and Potter, Pennsylvania* […]. Chicago: 1890.

Jones, Uriah. *History of the Early Settlement of the Juniata Valley.* Harrisburg, PA: Harrisburg Publishing, 1889, 253.

Kane Area Development Center. "History of Kane." https://kanepa.com.

Kane (PA) Republican. "Address of Robert Gray Taylor." January 9, 1934.

———. "Bennetts Valley Gas Boom." December 4, 1953.

———. "Centennial Scrapbook, Going Back in Time." December 29, 1969.

———. "Matter of Insurance Settlement Brought Up Once Famous Case." February 4, 1916.

———. "Yesterday's Dark Spell Similar to Phenomenon of 1780." September 25, 1950.

Keystone Elk Country Alliance. "Elk Country Visitor Center." https://experienceelkcountry.com/visitor-center/.

Kosack, Joe. "History of Pennsylvania Elk." Pennsylvania Game Commission. https://www.pgc.pa.gov/Wildlife/WildlifeSpecies/Elk/Pages/HistoryofElkinPA.aspx.

Lancaster (PA) Intelligencer. "75,000 Acres of Public Land." February 28, 1809.

Levine, Rich, and Bob Nay. "Bennetts Valley, Railroads, and the 'Hoodlebug.'" Mt. Zion Historical Society. https://mtzionhistoricalsociety.org/history/railroads/.

Library of Congress. "Castle Garden Bridge—Historic American Engineering Record, Cameron County Bridge No. 4, National Park Service."

Liquisearch. "Quehanna Wild Area—History—Atoms for Peace." https://www.liquisearch.com/.

———. "Quehanna Wild Area—History—State Forests." https://www.liquisearch.com/.

MacLean, Dougie. "Caledonia." Release date: 1978. https://genius.com/Dougie-maclean-caledonia-lyrics.

McKnight, J.W. *Pioneer Outline History of Northwest Pennsylvania.* Philadelphia: J.B. Lippencott, 1905.

Meginness, John F. *Journal of Samuel Maclay, While Surveying the West Branch of the Susquehanna, the Sinnemahoning and the Allegheny Rivers in 1790.* Williamsport, PA: Gazette and Bulletin, 1894.

Merriam-Webster. "Freshet." https://www.merriam-webster.com/dictionary/freshet.

Mt. Zion Historical Society. "The Cooking of Coal: A Bennett's Valley Legacy." Excerpts from the book *The Beehive Coke Years* by John K. Gates. https://mtzionhistoricalsociety.org/history/bennetts-valley/coal-and-coke/the-cooking-of-coal-a-bennetts-valley-legacy.

Mulvihill, Carol. "A Tribute to 'Freddy' the Famous Benezette Bull." *Endeavor News,* January 22, 2011.

National Archives. "Atoms for Peace." https://www.archives.gov.

National Park Service. "Treaty of Stanwix, Treaty & Land Transaction of 1784."

Nay, Bob. "Winslow Colliery Railroad and Reuben Winslow (1796–1871)." Mt. Zion Historical Society. https://mtzionhistoricalsociety.org/history/railroads/the-winslow-colliery-and-reuben-winslow/.

Nelson, Raymond. "Why Was It Called Benezette?" *Elk Horn* 33, no. 1 (Winter 1997): 3–4.

New Webster's Dictionary and Thesaurus. New York, 1991.

Olson, Eric Kincaid, II. "Kincaid Family Tree." https://www.ancestry.com.

PA Department of Conservation and Natural Resources. "About DCNR." https://www.dcnr.pa.gov/about/Pages/default.aspx.

———. "The Civilian Conservation Corps." https://www.dcnr.pa.gov/StateParks/History/CCCYears/Pages/default.aspx.

———. Hicks Run Civilian Conservation Camp, PA CCC On-line Archives.

———. "Sinnemahoning State Park." https://www.dcnr.pa.gov/StateParks/FindAPark/SinnemahoningStatePark/Pages/default.aspx.

———. "Teaberry Loop Trail."

PA Elk Country (blog). "Directions to the Cross and Chapel." http://paelkcountry.blogspot.com/2021/10/from-benezett-store-go-west-on-route.html.

Pearsall, Clarence Eugene. *History and Genealogy of the Pearsall Family in England and America.* Vol. 1. San Francisco: H.S. Crocker, 1928.

Penn Libraries, University of Pennsylvania. "James Potter, 1729–1789."

Pennsylvania Conservation Heritage Project. "Marion E. Brooks, 1912–1973." https://paconservationheritage.org/stories/marion-e-brooks/.

Pennsylvania Game Commission. "Elk." https://www.pgc.pa.gov/Education/WildlifeNotesindex/Pages/Elk.aspx.

———. "Elk Viewing Destinations." https://www.pgc.pa.gov/Wildlife/ WildlifeSpecies/Elk/Pages/ElkViewingDestinations.aspx.

Pennsylvania Great Outdoors Visitors Bureau. "Big Elk Lick Horse Campground." https://visitpago.com/listings/big-elk-lick-horse-camp/.

———."Bucktail Overlook." https://visitpago.com/listings/bucktail-overlook/.

———. "Discover Benezette, the Elk Capital of Pennsylvania." https://visitpago. com/counties/elk-county/benezette/.

———. "George B. Stevenson Reservoir." https://visitpago.com/listings/george-b-stevenson-reservoir/.

———. "Great Motorcycle Rides." May 9, 2023. https://visitpago.com/great-motorcycle-rides.

———. "Medix Hotel." https://visitpago.com/listings/medix-hotel.

———. "Mt. Zion Historical Park." May 5, 2020. https://visitpago.com/mt-zion-historical-park.

Pennsylvania Historic and Museum Commission. "Forty-Second Regiment (Bucktails) Pennsylvania Volunteers Records, Collection MG-234, Pennsylvania in the Civil War." https://www.phmc.pa.gov/.

———. "A Guide for Classroom Teachers Researching the Civil War at the Pennsylvania State Archives, Introduction." https://www.phmc.pa.gov/.

Pennsylvania Lumber Museum, "Explore the Lumber Heritage Region." https:// lumberheritage.org.

Pennsylvania State Grange. "Listing of Pennsylvania Granges (Charter Ledgers)." www.pagrange.org/listing-of-pennsylvania-granges-charter-ledgers.

Pennsylvania Wilds. "About the Pennsylvania Wilds." https://pawilds.com/about/.

———. "Quehanna Wild Area." https://pawilds.com/asset/quehanna.wild.area.

Philadelphia Inquirer. "Elk, PA's Largest Wild Animal, Have Become a Tourism Boom in the Northwest Part of the State." March 5, 2021.

Pittsburgh (PA) Dispatch. "Erasmus Morey." May 31, 1891.

Powell, Kimberly. "Castle Garden: America's First Official Immigration Center." ThoughtCo., updated on October 14, 2019. https://www.thoughtco.com/ castle-garden-americas-official-immigration-center-1422288.

Progress (Clearfield, PA). "Curtiss-Wright, Penn State Offer Special Opportunity to Young Men in Area." November 25, 1955.

———. "Day by Day Chronology of 1954's Top Area News." December 31, 1954.

———. "Elk Management Area Proposed." November 20, 1970.

———. "Landowners in Medix Run Carry Fight to Harrisburg." March 3, 1954.

———. "Landowners of Medix Run Protest Gas Boom Ruling." March 2, 1954.

———. "Man Made Rich by Gas Boom Dies." September 8, 1953.

———. "Monument, Forest Tract Honors Marion Brooks." October 3, 1975.

———. "State Sees Benezette Area Gas Boom Lasting Longer Than Leidy's." August 3, 1954.

Punxsutawney Area Historical & Genealogical Society. *Follow the Drinking Gourd*. A pamphlet by the Punxsutawney Area Historical & Genealogical Society.

Punxsutawney (PA) Spirit. "Minish Home Slave Pit Found Here." April 24, 1963.

Renovo (PA) Record. "The Oldest Settler on the West Branch, James Caldwell."
    March 4, 1875.

Ridgway (PA) Record. "Report of the Winslow Family Reunion." August 29, 1908.

Rogers, Fred M. *Rafting Days on the Loyalsock.* Published by the Lycoming Valley
    Historical Society, 1928.

Rootsweb. "John Barr." https://sites.rootsweb.com.

Rubinkam, Michael. "Witnesses to FBI Hunt in Elk County for Civil War Gold
    Describe What They Saw." Associated Press, updated October 8, 2023. https://
    wtaj.com/news/local/news/ap-witnesses-to-fbi-hunt-for-civil-war-gold.

scotthoskins. "U.S. History 1800–1817 Timeline." Timetoast Timelines. https://
    www.timetoast.com/timelines/us-history-1800-1817.

Secco, Marilyn. "Chapel Built in Benezette as a Memorial to Local Man's Father."
    Courier-Express (DuBois, PA), August 20, 2022.

Smrekar, Dan. "Memories." *Courier-Express* (DuBois, PA), September 25, 1974.

Taylor, Danielle. "Presidential Legends in the PA Great Outdoors Region."
    Pennsylvania Great Outdoors Visitors Bureau, February 19, 2019. https://
    visitpago.com/presidential-legends-in-the-pennsylvania-great-outdoors-region/.

Tokugawa Antiques. "A Brief History of the Larkin Soap Company Premiums."
    https://www.tokugawaantiques.com/a-brief-history-of-the-larkin-soap-
    company-premiums/.

U.S. Census Bureau. "Benezette Township, PA." 2020. www.census.gov.
    ———. "City and Town Population Totals, 2020–2021, Driftwood, PA." www.
    census.gov.

U.S. Energy Information Administration. "Pennsylvania State Energy Profile."
    https://www.eia.gov/state/print.php?sid=PA.

United States Gazette (Philadelphia). "30,000 Acres of Valuable Land." September
    24, 1817.

Valley Echo (Penfield, PA). "Morey." June 6, 1891.

Valley Girl Views (blog). "The Great Runaway of 1778." July 13, 2020. https://
    susquehannavalley.blogspot.com/2020/07/the-great-runaway.html.

Valley Sentinel (Carlisle, PA). "Love and Jealousy." June 30, 1876.

Wallace, Paul A.W. *Conrad Weiser, 1696–1760, Friend of Colonist and Mohawk.*
    Philadelphia: University of Pennsylvania Press, 1945.
    ———. *Indians in Pennsylvania.* Harrisburg: Commonwealth of Pennsylvania, the
    Pennsylvania Historic and Museum Commission, 1964.

Weidenboerner, Katie. "Historian Shocked FBI Searching Dents Run, Warns
    about Findings." *Courier-Express* (DuBois, PA), March 15, 2018.

Wessman, Alice L. *A History of Elk County, Pennsylvania, 1981.* Ridgway, PA: Elk
    County Historical Society, 1981.

West, Dan. "Elk County: Stations of the Past." Pennsylvania Railroad Stations
    Past and Present, West 2K. https://www.west2k.com/pastations/elk.shtml.

Williamsport (PA) Sun-Gazette. "The Story of Fred, Gentle Giant." March 20, 2011.

Winslow House Heritage Council. *The History Lessons of a Schoolgirl, Miss Victoria
    Winslow, Benezette, Elk County, PA.* Winslow House Heritage Council, 2007.

ABOUT THE AUTHOR

Kathy Myers is a native of Ridgway, Elk County, Pennsylvania, where she has spent most of her life. She was the director of marketing at Elk County General Hospital in Ridgway and, prior to her retirement, was the owner of Area Abstracting and Filing Service, a real estate settlement/title abstract company serving attorneys in Clearfield and Jefferson Counties.

A member of the seventh generation of her family to live in the Wilds, Myers is a historian, genealogist and writer who now resides in the Beechwoods of Jefferson County. She is a member of the General Society of Mayflower Descendants (GSMD), the founder and past governor of the Winslow Heritage Society and a member of the DuBois Area Historical Society.

She has published pieces in local newspapers; in the *Mayflower Quarterly*, an international publication; and in a local literary publication and has authored *Historic Tales of the Pennsylvania Wilds* and *The Pennsylvania Wilds and the Civil War*, both published by The History Press.

Myers served her community as president of the Ridgway Area School Board, president of the Elk County General Hospital Auxiliary and president of the Elk County Recreation and Tourist Council. She served on the GSMD 2014 Congress Planning Committee, was a chairperson of the GSMD Marketing Committee and served as membership chair for the Society of Mayflower Descendants in Pennsylvania, where she also acted as assistant to the historian. She was regent of the DuBois-Susquehanna Chapter of the Daughters of the American Revolution.

She is married to her high school sweetheart, John, and they are the parents of one son and have two grandsons.

Visit us at
www.historypress.com
....